BLACK
AND
WHITE

PAT BROWN

BLACK
AND
WHITE

HOW THE LEFT IS
DESTROYING THE DREAM OF
MARTIN LUTHER KING, JR.
AND OUR FOUNDING FATHERS

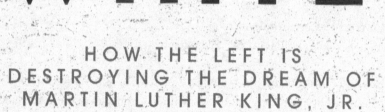

DAVE BROWN

Post Hill
PRESS

A POST HILL PRESS BOOK
ISBN: 978-1-64293-681-0
ISBN (eBook): 978-1-64293-682-7

Black and White:
How the Left is Destroying the Dream of Martin Luther King, Jr. and our
Founding Fathers
© 2021 by Pat Brown and Dave Brown
All Rights Reserved

Cover art by Cory Corcoran
Authors' photos by Tami Cicale Photography

Post Hill Press
New York • Nashville
posthillpress.com

Published in the United States of America
1 2 3 4 5 6 7 8 9 10

To all Americans who are fighting to save our country.

TABLE OF CONTENTS

DISCLAIMER

Pat and Dave Brown aren't haters. We don't hate people. What we hate are destructive ideas and the danger these ideas pose to our country. We love people of all colors, all cultures, all religions, and all lifestyles, but we object to the parts of any culture, religion, or lifestyle that harms other people, especially children. We are conservatives, and yes, we have supported President Trump because we have found him to be a president who is willing to work with both sides of the aisle and compromise where it is necessary to keep our country from crashing and burning. We don't think all Democrats are bad or all Republicans good, and we aren't in favor of a one-party system. We want good representatives from both parties to work together to preserve and improve a country that was built on the most brilliant document ever written: the Constitution. We want life, liberty, and happiness for all our citizens, not just ourselves and the people we are buddies with. But we a see a frightening swing to the far left with a level of bizarre behaviors and thinking that seem to be going mainstream. We think conservatives, especially those toward the middle—heck, even liberals toward the middle—need to start addressing the problem of what is happening to our country. We need to be "woke" too—just not the kind of "woke" the Left wants us to be.

OUR CLAN

Yeah, we have one—just not one that starts with a K, although people of the Left tend to like to throw that word around and connect it with any white person (or even black person) who doesn't agree with them. Our clan is a jumble of races and cultures. Pat Brown's father Harry, Dave's grandfather, was one of the last Jews to escape Germany before no more could emigrate. A teen when he came to America, he lived with his parents and brother in New York City where he learned perfect English and spoke it without an accent. He eventually became a citizen, joined the Navy, and became an electronic engineer. After a decade of working in New York laboratories and living across the bridge in northern New Jersey, he moved the family to McLean, Virginia, and spent the remainder of his career working for the assistant secretary of the Navy at the Pentagon and for NASA. He worked on a lot of secret stuff, but he never divulged anything about the work to his family. He never discussed religion or politics.

Pat's mother Shirley, Dave's grandmother, grew up an only child of New England Presbyterians, daughter of a paper mill worker and a housewife. In the summers, they lived on a houseboat where each morning, Stanley took the motorboat to work, leaving his wife, Doris, and daughter, Shirley, alone on the boat until evening. It was in these lonely hours that Shirley became an artist, eventually selling thousands of watercolors depicting the landscapes of her youth. After a wild year of traveling as a performer with the Ice Capades, Shirley married Harry and settled down to paint and be a stay-at-home mother (as was expected in the 1950s). Pat was one of three children, all girls, the baby of the family.

On the Brown side of Dave's family—their names are not going to be mentioned here due to the present day doxxing problem and the fact that they may not approve of everything written in this book or particularly approve of Dave and Pat's political opinions—their story begins in the parish of Clarendon, just northwest of Kingston in Jamaica. Actually, one of his great-grandmothers was born in Cuba, but both his father's parents were born and raised in Jamaica.

It was a hard life, working the land as farmers and raising six children, of which David's father was the eldest. Wishing a better life for their children, Dave's grandfather came to the US and worked as a farm laborer. Then his grandmother followed and became a caretaker for families in DC. Both were legal immigrants.

Dave's father arrived here in the US at the age of fifteen. He graduated high school in Washington, DC, and joined his father working in the mailroom of *National Geographic* while his mother worked in the janitorial services at a local hospital. He became a citizen and, at the age of nineteen, met and married Pat Brown. They were married for twenty-five years. Dave has one biracial sister and an adopted black brother. He grew up in Berwyn Heights, Maryland, a predominately white blue collar town during his childhood. He got along just fine there, as did his brother and sister.

Now, Pat lives in Bowie, Maryland, one of the wealthiest black communities in the US, near the other two kids and Dave lives on Maryland's Eastern shore. They have aunts, uncles, nieces, nephews, grandkids, and in-laws of all colors, and no one cares in the family. We are just family.

The family is also a jumble of professions. Pat Brown is a criminal profiler, TV commentator, and author. Dave's dad is a service engineer. Dave is a small business owner. Their relatives are white, brown, and black, college-educated and high school-was-enough-educated. They work in education, law, public service, hospitality, finance, music, and construction. They are not all in agreement on political matters or who they voted for or will vote for in the next election. Their friends come in all colors, practice different religions, have different sexual orientations, and are from different countries. Pat and Dave are poster people for the Democratic Party! Except they are conservatives. Once upon a time, the Democratic Party had positions that they were not totally opposed to and when they had reasonable stances on certain issues, they might even vote for a particular local Democratic candidate. But because of the dangerous direction that the Democratic Party has gone, Pat and Dave now find little common ground with their current platform. This book will show why this is happening and why more people leaning left should start veering right.

CHAPTER ONE

WHITE WOMEN YOGA
THE UGLY TRUTH OF
A CLANDESTINE RACE WAR

"Injustice anywhere is a threat to justice everywhere."
MARTIN LUTHER KING, JR.[1]

A few years before Martin Luther King, Jr. was assassinated, the landmark Civil Rights Act of 1964 was passed. The Act was the crowning achievement of a brutal civil rights war and the shining example of Dr. King's dramatic and heartfelt cry to the crowds on the Mall in Washington, DC, in 1963, when he proclaimed:

> I have a dream that one day this nation will rise up and live out the true meaning of its creed: "We hold these truths to be self-evident, that all men are created equal."
>
> I have a dream that one day on the red hills of Georgia, the sons of former slaves and the sons of for-

---

1. Mindock, Clark. "Martin Luther King Jr: 50 quotes from the civil rights leader who inspired a nation." *Independent*. Last modified January 20, 2020. https://www.independent.co.uk/news/world/americas/martin-luther-king-quotes-death-assassination-mlk-jr-a8855071.html.

mer slave owners will be able to sit down together at the table of brotherhood.

I have a dream that my four little children will one day live in a nation where they will not be judged by the color of their skin but by the content of their character. I have a dream today.

I have a dream that one day…little black boys and black girls will be able to join hands with little white boys and white girls as sisters and brothers. I have a dream today.[2]

Although there would be more battles to fight to ensure that no person would be discriminated against in our great country, to ensure that all our citizens had the opportunity to exercise their right to pursue liberty and happiness without being limited by their skin color or their place of birth, the Civil Rights Act of 1964 was a huge leap forward in achieving this goal. Finally, no business could hang out a sign that said, "Whites Only," and no one who served the public could close their door to citizens simply because they did not wish to associate with people of a different race, color, religion, sex, or national origin. Although it took years to enforce the law, certainly by the year 2019, it was assumed that all citizens could go to any place of public accommodation (a store, a restaurant, a golf club, and so on) and not worry about being turned away at the door.

Or so it seemed. Quietly growing under the cover of being sensitive to marginalized groups of people, violations of the Civil Rights Act of 1964 were increasing, and many people did not recognize this un-American discrimination as illegal

2. King, Martin L. "I Have a Dream." Yale Law School. Speech presented August 28, 1963. http://avalon.law.yale.edu/20th_century/mlk01.asp.

and immoral, but rather quietly accepted the "slight" and looked the other way. This has been the modus operandi of the silent majority since the 1964 Act. Occasionally, someone might break from this mold to protest the hypocrisy, but then they are browbeaten back into silence, which, in turn, further discourages others who might speak up as well. Unfortunately, permitting these ostensibly benign acts of discrimination to go on unaddressed has allowed a small flame to grow into a raging inferno. No longer are we seeing just small pockets of minorities forming groups on their own as they seek to socialize with those of a similar culture or deal with local issues in their communities, as has been common in past years; now they are being encouraged to do so in very militant and sometimes illegal fashion by the so-called intellectual elites, many of whom are white. Think about it! White liberals promoting segregation in 2019! But you can only push people so far before their anger and frustration begin to outweigh the ostracism they might face. We may have finally reached that point.

PAT

I was one of those people. I suppose when one attended a heavily white college and a black student union existed on campus, it was easy to accept that a minority might try to make their voices heard, to share their ideas with the greater population, to speak up so as not to be invisible. With the civil rights movement not too far in the rearview mirror, it seemed only right to not object to black students or Latino students or Chinese students gathering separately if they wished to have a club or a society or a fraternity or sorority inclusive to only their own. It was just something one didn't find particularly offensive considering the times, especially when one is young and easily influenced by whatever is the predominant thinking on their college campus.

But, by 2019, and long out of the university environment, I expected that I lived in a world where the Civil Rights Act of 1964 applied to my town, my county, my state, my country. I didn't have any issue with people of a particular race gathering together, families and friends who happen to be racially similar meeting up; it is normal for people to hang with whom they are closest to by relation or culture. But I never thought that public one-race groups would be advertised and promoted as just that—groups that specifically told persons of another color they were not allowed to participate. Certainly, when I ran a couple of Meetup groups—these are groups one pays Meetup for to have the right to provide a service to the public and for which one may require fees for membership, for special events, or for classes—I didn't think racial prejudice would be welcomed as a part of the mix. Once one has rented a "storefront" on the Meetup website, Meetup will advertise the group to the general public and invite Meetup members to partake of the group's services. Naturally, I thought *all* members would be accepted. My groups were *Relaxed Maryland Walkers* and *Older Women, Cheap Travel. Relaxed Maryland Walkers* included both male and female members who joined the walks I planned throughout the region. Naturally, any race was welcome. Barring people who were not white like me never crossed my mind. Depending on the location of the walk, more whites might participate or more blacks might participate. The racial makeup tended to fall along the lines of the neighborhood in which the walk was conducted. *Older Women, Cheap Travel* also included all races, and the makeup of the races aligned with the country visited; the trip to Cuba was particularly popular with black women, and so this was the trip I ran that had far more blacks than whites.

Never when I created my groups did I think I could exclude or would want to exclude anyone based on their race, the color of their skin, their national origin, or their religion. Yes, *Older Women, Cheap Travel* was for women because we were sharing hotel rooms (and "older" was in the description to let younger women know that this wasn't a party tour or a tour with a lot of walking and hiking and extreme sports). The issue of separation of the sexes is always a bit sticky because while the Civil Rights Act of 1964 doesn't allow discrimination based on sex, there are accommodations for places like restrooms, gyms, and other specific situations where it might be acceptable to have separation of males and females (although there are those who would argue this point).

I ran my groups successfully, and I joined other Meetup groups to participate in various activities I enjoyed. Now that I was on their mailing list, I began to receive a particular kind of email that I pretty much ignored when they first started showing up in my mailbox. But when these emails started coming in regularly, I began to be a little disturbed. Here was Meetup advertising these groups to me, encouraging me to join these groups, and yet, the names of these groups included one of the following words or phrases: black, African American, POC (people of color), melanin, sisters, and ADOS (American descendants of slaves). These weren't groups focusing on some political issue; these were groups like my walking and traveling groups. There was *Sisters with Suitcases, Black Girls Lift, Black Women who want more DC, Black Travelers Network, Black Unicorns, Black Nonbelievers of DC, Black Girl Clique, Mahogany*

Travelers, Black Technologists, Black Women of a Certain age, Well-Read Black Girls of Maryland, Sassy but Classy Sista Circle, and *Yoga is for Black Girls,* just to name a dozen Meetups out of hundreds.

Some of these Meetup groups allowed one to join without being approved. Interestingly, when I scanned the photos of the members of these kinds of groups, to be sure, pretty much everyone was a person of color. It seemed that since the group made it clear that only one race was welcome, other races simply did not sign up. As to the groups that required one to submit a request to become a member, I was declined by all of the groups I tried to join. What was the reason? It was simply my photo that came along with my request. When I asked some of the moderators why I was rejected, I was told a number of times that the group was for people of African American descent only. When I asked what percentage I would need to be able to join, I did not receive an answer. Clearly, if one looked white, one couldn't join, which meant even a person who is three-quarters white and one-quarter black (what used to be called quadroon) would not be able to join even though she was of African American descent—just not enough African American descent and too white in appearance to be accepted. This led me to coin a new word: PONEC, or a person of not enough color. Because if a person will be accepted because they are a POC—a person of color—it seems to be the opposite for PONEC, as they will be often be excluded by blacks and other POC unless they serve a useful purpose to be included (like saying biracial Barack Obama is black because that will make him the first black president and quadroon Meghan Markle is a person of color because that means a POC has finally become the Duchess of Sussex). But if a mixed-race person looks too white and serves no political purpose, they might be just a PONEC who POC reject.

Meetup has been in business for almost two decades, and they sold it to WeWork in 2017 for 156 million dollars.[3] Here is a blurb from Wikipedia that does not include the issue of one-race-only groups that have been permitted since the earliest days of Meetup and still exist into 2021 as this book came into publication.

> Meetup is an online service used to create groups that host local in-person events. As of 2017, there are about 35 million Meetup users. Each user can be a member of multiple groups or RSVP for any number of events. Users are usually using the website to find friends, share a hobby, or for professional networking. Meetup users do not have "followers" or other direct connections with each other like on other social media sites.
>
> Meetup users self-organize into groups. As of 2017, there are about 225,000 Meetup groups in 180 countries. Each group has a different topic, size, and rules. Groups are associated with one of 30+ categories and any number of more than 18,000 tags that identify the group's theme. The most popular categories are "adventure and outdoor activities, career and business, and parents and family." Most events are on a structured schedule each week or month at a local venue, typically on evenings or weekends.

3.　Newcomb, Alyssa, "Meetup was a darling of the tech industry. But can it survive WeWork?" NBC News. Accessed July 12, 2020. https://www.nbcnews.com/tech/tech-news/meetup-was-darling-tech-industry-can-it-survive-wework-n1106676.

Meetup groups are run by approximately 140,000 organizers. Any Meetup user can be an organizer. Organizers set up groups, organize events, and develop event content. They also pay a fee to run the group, under the expectation of sharing the cost with members that attend events. Meetup has policies against organizing meetups around a commercial interest, hate speech, or groups that do not meet in-person. This policy, against organizing meetups around commercial interests is not only not enforced; but, the Meetup company intentionally and deliberately ignore the policy and allow such to become Meetup groups. About 28% of organizers have sponsors that provide venues, drinks, and event content. [4]

No one has complained about the race issue. I found this astounding since Meetup seems to me to be in clear violation of the Civil Rights Act of 1964 under Title II (Public Accommodations).[5] I decided to confront them. I sent a Tweet and asked them:

I am a white woman who lives in the DC area (Prince George's Country, Maryland) and I have found I am locked out of many dozens of groups in my area because the organizers label the groups as Black, African American, Mahogany, People of Color, etc. in a manner which clearly seems to be a way of keeping white people

4.   Wikipedia. "Meetup." Last modified August 3, 2020. https://en.wikipedia.org/wiki/Meetup.

5.   The United States Department of Justice. "Title II of the Civil Rights Act (Public Accommodations)." Civil Rights Division. Last modified October 11, 2016. https://www.justice.gov/crt/title-ii-civil-rights-act-public-accommodations.

from joining. These are women's groups, travel groups, photography groups, etc., which should have no need to attach race to joining requirements.

Meetup responded with:

We believe there is a Meetup group for everyone, Pat. We'd love to help you find one that works for you. Let us know if we can help!

I tweeted back:

I think you are totally ignoring the issue which is against your policy (which I thought was true at the time of this tweet) and is discrimination. I live in a majority black community and I am being refused admission to a great many Meetups due to race.[6]

And Meetup tweeted back:

Meetup fosters communities of people centered on interests or common identities. Meetup is a diverse community and group identities can be centered around gender, race, religion, political affiliations, or language among many other things.[7]

I was floored. Meetup was actually telling me that one-race-only groups were not against policy and were permissible. And yet they tweeted out to the general public, "Meetup condemns

---

6. Brown, Pat. "I think you are totally ignoring the issue." Twitter post, January 21, 2019. https://twitter.com/profilerpatb/status/1087465397572517891?s=21.

7. Meetup Support. "Meetup fosters communities of people centered on interests." Twitter post, January 21, 2019. https://twitter.com/meetup_support/status/1087460 164503040001?s=21.

racism, white supremacy, and every other form of hate and bigotry. Learn more about our hate policy."[8] Rather contradictory, eh? So I pursued.

> So, what you are saying, since I cannot join groups that require me to be a POC, I can start White Photographers, White Women Travel, and White DC Socializers?[9]

Meetup did not respond.

Then they blocked me.

Now frustration and curiosity got the better of me. I wanted to test Meetup's commitment to one-race-only groups and see if an all-white group would actually be permitted and how it would be received. I googled and found only one other person had tried this back in 2011 and that group was roundly attacked and quickly removed from Meetup.[10] So, I knew when I committed to this experiment, I was likely going to be setting myself up as a target. But at least as the mother of three non-white children and a person who has spent much of her life around people of other races and cultures, it would be more difficult for people to accuse me of being a racist or a white supremacist (or so I thought), and my years of being a media personality had toughened me so that when the hate started flying my way, I could withstand the assault. If someone was going to make an issue of this violation of the Civil Rights Act, I might as well be the one to do it.

---

8. Meetup. "Meetup condemns racism, white supremacy, and every other form of hate." Twitter post, August 17, 2017. https://twitter.com/meetup/status/898318516474040325?s=21.

9. Brown, Pat. "So, what you are saying, since I cannot join groups." Twitter post, January 21, 2019. https://twitter.com/profilerpatb/status/1087465708810842118?s=21.

10. Herbert, Erin. "Whites-Only Meetup.com Group is Canceled." *American Renaissance*. Last modified September 8, 2011. https://www.amren.com/news/2011/09/whites-only_mee/.

So, I started three groups: *White Women Walkers, Caucasian Camera Buffs,* and *European-American Culture Club,* none of which had a restricted membership. Would only whites apply like I saw happen with the blacks-only Meetups that did not require approval for new members? Would Meetup object? Would people write to me or Meetup to complain I was running racist groups? I set up my first Meetups for each group with a specific time and location (that I had no intention of actually following through on).

Interestingly, the *European-American Culture Club* got little attention. The *Caucasian Camera Buffs,* however, had quite a few black men join who then wrote me with complaints about the name of the group. It was clear they only "joined" to send me angry emails. *White Women Walkers* got the most members, and almost all of them were POC or white liberals who each sent me a scathing message about setting up the group. Some said they were reporting me to Meetup for discrimination. Some called the Meetup a hate group. Some said they would gather all their friends who were POC and meet me at the designated location for the first *White Women Walkers* Meetup to confront me. I bet that would have ended up on YouTube!

Is this for real? Do you mean white as in Caucasian? Excluding others?

If I were ½ Caucasian mixed with African, Latino, Asian, Indian blood, would I be excluded?

I'm just going to assume the host is a Game of Thrones fan and meant Women White Walkers because the other obvious interpretation is just disgusting.

What the heck? At this moment in history you think it's a good idea to call a Meetup group White Women Walkers? You may want to rethink.

On the bright side, now we know who the racists are so we don't accidentally try to befriend you!!

So glad there's a group for white women so they can sit around & talk about how hard it is to be surrounded by poor, uneducated brown folk!

I can't wait to bring all of my black, Asian and Middle Eastern friends to the first walk! Woohoo!!!

This is extremely racist. Embarrassing.

You can't be serious. White women?

You have to be joking you racist pos!

WTF, is there a way to report this to an administrator?

Then, there was the woman who concluded that everything I have done in life is to put down people of color and to control them. I had no idea I was so subversive!

As a minority member I have dealt with people like this woman. Bring her into your group and she'll think she's supposed to lead it and set the agenda even when the group has already set one. This woman is so intent on changing the black agenda that she married black, and had black children that she home schooled to prove to black people that she is better at raising kids. Blacks and other minorities want no part of this unique kind of racist. They can be the most toxic kind of all.

Of course, there was the leftist intellectual who came through to educate me.

Black women and other marginalized groups have experienced and continue to experience shared trauma. These groups are fully entitled to prefer time to get away from members of groups that historically and continue to oppress and marginalize them. White people as a group have suffered no collective harm from people of color, and there is no benefit to whites of participating in white-only groups besides racism and upholding white supremacy.

Someone needs to remind this person that the Civil Rights Act of 1964 didn't have a "shared trauma" clause that allowed specific groups to not comply.

So, I wrote Meetup with my concerns and received this reply from their "Integrity Specialist":

Hi Pat,

As an organizer you are welcome to monitor your memberships. This means you are free to admit or deny members at your discretion.

As mentioned previously, we allow groups to come together based on a common identity. If a member wants to create a group to connect with their ethnicity, be it Black, Asian, or what have you, they are more than welcome to do so.

There is nothing wrong with people wanting to meet other people and create a private space with others who share a similar culture or identity.

This includes you. If you feel the need to have a private space to connect with other white folks, you are allowed to do so.

Now bear in mind, and this applies to all groups regardless of their identities, within your description, we recommend refraining from mentioning who you do not allow (emphasis theirs). Rather, we recommend focusing on who you do allow (emphasis theirs).

Regarding members who complain against you, I highly recommend refraining from engaging them, and instead remove them from your group.

Thank you again for understanding our policies.

Best,
Dwayne
Senior Integrity Specialist
Meetup HQ

I found quite a number of things in this communication to be an issue.

1. While I agree that people have the right "to create a private place with others who share a similar culture or identity, there is nothing private about Meetup. A private place would be gathering with friends at your home or another's home or renting a place where you are having a private event (such as a wedding or a birthday party) or, one could say, even a private table at a park for a Fourth of July picnic. In none of these cases is one advertising to the general public or providing an event for a fee to the general public. In other words, Meetup is hardly simply renting out a private space for you to then send invitations out to only your friends to come and participate. Meetup is advertising, just as one would in a newspaper, to all the subscribers to come and join in an event bringing together strangers, not friends. These are businesses, through and through, with money exchanging hands in order to conduct these businesses. And they meet in physical locations, most often public physical locations.

2. "Refrain from mentioning who you do not allow but rather focus on who you *do* allow." In other words, you can't hang out a "No Blacks Permitted" sign, but you can hang out a "Whites Only" sign. Is it only me, or isn't this the exact type of thing that the civil rights movement fought so hard to end?

3. It is recommended that I don't engage members who complain against me (I sent a standard reply to each stating that my Meetup was an approved group and got reprimanded for that for reasons I still fail to understand). I am curious what Meetup would have done if they continued to be swamped with complaints about my groups and this had made it into the media as Meetup sponsoring a hate group. Unfortunately, I will never exactly know what would have happened because Meetup pulled my groups after reading my blog on the experiment with the claim they were not legitimate groups but fake groups to test their policies (well, they were correct about that, so I cannot argue that point).

While I was communicating with Meetup over the legitimacy of my three groups, I ran across *Yoga is 4 Black Girls* and read the description with great interest. This group was blatant in their separatist leanings.

This MeetUp group is to allow space for Black women together in the name of yoga, surrounded by the supportive community of Black people, Black yoga instructors, and all around safe Black spaces.

In this group, we attend, primarily, yoga classes and build one another up all while debunking the idea that yoga is not for us.

The goal: more yoga mats in the hands of Black women, men, and children! [11]

Interesting. So, since my *European-American Culture Club* wasn't getting much traffic, I dropped it and substituted *White Women Yoga* using exactly the same wording, changing out black for white.

This MeetUp group is to allow space for White women together in the name of yoga, surrounded by the supportive community of White people, White yoga instructors, and all around safe White spaces.

My email box exploded!

Are you kidding me? Appalling. Reported and I hope your group is taken down immediately.

You cannot establish a group based on race, color or ethnicity and restrict "everyone", that's called Racism and it should not be allowed on this platform

I agree but why is no one complaining about the POC groups? Oh, I forgot. They get ignore the law.

This is unbelievably racist.

So do you have to be 100% white? Is a DNA test required to prove you are related to Adolph Hitler?

You're a dumb racist. I hope you feel unsafe in your ignorant Klan meetup.

I thought yoga was for everyone.

---

11.   Meetup. "Yoga is 4 Black Girls." Last modified January 22, 2019. https://www. meetup.com/Yoga-is-4-Black-Girls/.

Hey CNN: How you gonna let Pat Brown, the racist bigot, be a commentator for you? I have called your call center 22 times, the operators are just instantly hanging up on me. I guess no one at your organization cares about the fact that your employee is an openly racist bigot? No worries, the social media assault is on! I will find you and everyone of your anchors, until someone wants to talk about it.

You are a disgusting human being; we will shut you down.

Is this a joke? What about brown/tan/non-white bodies is scary? Do you realize that yoga was created by brown people? This is insulting on so many levels. No one who has studied yoga would find this to be acceptable.

This group is so sad. I can't believe how hateful and racist you are. You do realize that yoga originated in India, a country full of people of color. People like you are the reason the US is in such turmoil. Where's the love for your fellow (wo)man. I'm so disappointed in you.

And, of course, I got educated because obviously I must be ignorant as all get out (since I am white) and totally afraid of POC.

Hi Pat! What inspired you to create a yoga group for only white women? White women have safe spaces to gather everywhere in this world. What is it about being around black, brown, indigenous individuals that makes you feel unsafe? Especially considering that yoga as a traditional and spiritual practice comes from the Indian community. It feels concerning in the least to take this practice and then refuse to allow the exact people it culturally came from any access to the community. Can I be honest and say something that might hurt? It's racist. Please delete the group and learn a bit and open your heart as soon as possible.

I was quite amused when I received anger from people accusing me of being racist and having no clue about yoga and India. At that time, I was wearing a sari and hanging out with all POC: I was spending the entire month in India, and I was the only white person I had seen from the time I left the airport until the time I returned to the airport. Oddly, the kind woman who wrote above does not seem to think black people need to open their hearts and let white and Indian people into their classes. Is that not being racist and committing cultural appropriation without any regard for where one got the practice from? Apparently not. It's only bad when white people act that way.

I also find it very frustrating when I am told that since I have white people I can go hang out with, why am I trying to get into black groups? Couldn't we say that to black people too? Go away and go hang out with your own kind. How racist is that?! Does anyone understand that just because one is a certain color, it does not automatically confer a comfort level? There are many groups of white women I have little in common with and am totally uncomfortable hanging out with. To tell the truth, because I have been in so many groups of people over my lifetime that were not white people, I feel far more comfortable, in general, with cultures attached to people of other races. So isn't being forced to only associate with people of one's color a racist concept?

I live in a community that is only 13 percent white—exactly the same percentage of blacks in the United States population.[12] So, in Prince George's County, Maryland, I *am* the minority. When I go shopping, to the bank, out to eat, or to participate in community events, I *am* one of the few whites in the room and, often, the only white. I am not uncomfortable at all with this, probably because none of my kids are white, my ex-husband wasn't white, and I have so many friends from other countries outside of Europe. I have a great time playing pickleball in our very racially mixed league, and I love dancing at one of our local line dance groups, where I am indeed the only white person because the music is soul and R&B and the whole community surrounding the location is pretty much 100 percent African American.

And then here comes Meetup, who tells me if groups in my area refuse me due to race, it is not a problem because I can just drive an extra half an hour to be in a Meetup that accepts white people!

What is wrong with this picture?

DAVE

"You might be getting a call from *The Washington Post*." That is what I was told when my mother phoned me late one evening. "If you want to give a statement, great, go ahead. And if not, that's 100 percent fine, too." Of course, this pertained to her

---

12.   Maryland Demographics. "Is Prince George's Country the Best Maryland County for your Business?" Accessed July 17, 2020. https://www.maryland-demographics.com/prince-george-s-county-demographics; United States Census Bureau. "Quick Facts." Accessed July 17, 2020. https://www.census.gov/quickfacts/fact/table/US/PST045219.

own interview with the *Post* regarding her cheeky new Meetup group, *White Women Yoga*. For most, this might be an unusual call to get, but for my siblings and I, this was about par for the course. My mother has never been shy about voicing her opinion, regardless of whoever it might upset. But this was different as I could be involved personally. What would I say? "No comment; please don't contact me again"? Or would I spend the next half hour pouring out all my thoughts and opinions? As it turns out, I never had to make that decision. The phone call never came. My mother didn't give them my number, and I guess they couldn't find me because my name is not very unusual. But what would I have said? Well, the issue wasn't really about any reluctance to voice my opinion but whether it would be properly represented. Based on what I have seen over the last couple of years, my faith in fair reporting by the media has been tainted, and knowing what I would say, I doubted if what I said would be accurately reported. Here, however, I can say exactly what feel, without a filter, directly to you, the reader. I hope you will indulge me.

Like many of you, I have very strong feelings about our magnificent country. Not a day goes by that I don't thank God for having had the luck of being born here. Yet, day after day, I see it being torn down by those who historically have been the most advantaged. Here I am, a person of color, living my life free and how I see fit. I'm not angry, frustrated, or resentful, but apparently, I should be. In fact, I should be living in fear! Around every corner is a racist cop, an angry bigot, a privileged white person whose constant slights should be eating away at my soul. How is it I am content, and yet there is a young white college student living in the same country who believes we're a heartbeat away from the Fourth Reich? We live in crazy times, and it seems it's the crazy people who do the most talking. That's why I want to get my two cents in. If I'm anything like you, I have generally bit my lip and kept quiet, but I think I've had enough of that. We are way down that rabbit hole, and I fear we are no longer in a position where we can grind our teeth and swallow our tongues. Yes, we are the silent majority, but I don't think we can remain so any longer. I include myself as being among you; I am male, conservative, and biracial, but most importantly, I'm an American. I do, however, hope I can use my background to bring some real honesty to the forefront.

Isn't that what the Left always says? That they want to have an open and honest discussion about race? That is why I have chosen to join with my mother to write this book. This isn't the black experience or the white experience; this is both of those experiences blended together to give our unique perspective of race relations in our country today. For you normal Americans, I think you will find our viewpoint refreshing, and for the "progressive" Left, I can only imagine.

PAT

Luckily, there were many who were happy with my Meetup experiment. After my story appeared in the (very slanted to the left) *Washington Post* article, many people read my blogs on the matter. Then after I appeared on *Tucker Carlson* to discuss the issue, I got these kinds of responses that gave me hope!

> I'm not sure what I'm allowed to say these days. I hope you write a book…it is needed.
>
> ~Rebecca

I LOVE YOU!!!!! I love you!!!!...The fact that your MEETUP will get this kind of media attention, while the others did not...should be a huge red flag as to the broken laws that are overlooked to keep down a race issue. I am totally against discrimination, and totally for treating everyone as equal and have been since the 70s.

~Omelia

I saw your interview with Tucker Carlson last night. Thank you so much for so expertly exposing our society to the contradictory practice of all other groups, events or meetings for a select class of people being acceptable unless it's white. I live in Los Angeles; I see this every day and it saddens me. I hope your interview last night gets millions of shares and people wake up!!!!! Thank you, thank you, thank you!!!!!

~Heather

One thing, about this separatism is for those us that look like one race but are multiracial...we don't fit into any race...cause to deny one aspect is to deny the rest of oneself.

~Tamatha

"In a time of deceit, telling the truth is a revolutionary act" – George Orwell, author of "Animal Farm" and also "1984". Ms. Brown, you certainly have chosen a subject that will not see much support from the media. The Washington Post article conveniently left out supporting facts, but I am not surprised. I am also fairly certain that you are not that surprised at the reactions you have elicited with your online experiment.

I understand your motivation in this matter, for your children and grandchildren; I stand with you also to continue the motivation of my own children and grandchildren, to bring us TOGETHER, not to grow apart.

~Michael

Pat, I appreciate your effort in establishing the White Yoga group and shedding light on the segregation in this country and the obvious double standards. It amazes me others do not see it. The people opposing it are using the same words segregationists used over 50 years ago. Keep up the good work. There are millions who support your work. I am white and have absolutely been discriminated against, as have my children. Those that say we don't understand show their own bias and ignorance. Thank you.

~Josh

Pat, I read your story and was moved to thank you for being brave enough to cleverly raise a mirror to the face of true racism. Those who attack your words are either too angry and/or too ignorant to comprehend the satire of White Women Yoga. You words are so well stated that maybe, just maybe, it will cause people to take a moment to think about what a racial mess is being created in America and cause someone else to speak out against the ugly and dangerous rhetoric of racism in a manner as honest and as eloquent as you have. Kind regards.

~David

We are out here, white and black, POAC (People of ALL colors), and we need to stand up and be heard and take action.

CHAPTER TWO

RACISM TO RACIALISM AND BACK TO RACISM

"Black supremacy is as dangerous as white supremacy, and God is not interested merely in the freedom of black men. God is interested in the freedom of the whole human race and in the creation of a society where all men can live together as brothers."

MARTIN LUTHER KING, JR. [1]

PAT

I rewatched *Guess Who's Coming to Dinner* the other day, a movie I had not seen in decades. I had to admit I was impressed with this 1967 movie that came out only three years after the Civil Rights Act of 1964. It was not only well-acted, with Sidney Poitier, Katharine Hepburn, and Spencer Tracy in the lead parts, but it was sensitive, realistic, and evenhanded. The question at that moment in time was, all things being equal, if the fiancé were a fine upstanding man with a good education and a successful career, would you care if your white daughter

---

1. Mindock, Clark. "Martin Luther King Jr: 50 quotes from the civil rights leader who inspired a nation." *Independent.* Last modified January 20, 2020. https://www.independent.co.uk/news/world/americas/martin-luther-king-quotes-death-assassination-mlk-jr-a8855071.html.

married a black man? And if you had concerns, were you a racist or a realist?

The question brought me back to 1971 when, at my karate school, I met a handsome black man, Willie, who asked me for a date. I was but seventeen years old, and I think he must have been ten years older. At any rate, I accepted, and he came to my McLean, Virginia, all-white neighborhood to pick me up. My parents appeared as taken aback as did the white parents in the film who were surprised when their daughter brought a black fiancé to dine with them. I went out, and when I arrived home, my parents told me I could not go out with him again.

I was angry. I yelled at them. I must have been aware of racial issues of the time and the rarity at that point in our country's history of interracial dating, but I had never heard a negative, racist word from my parents over nonwhite people; in fact, the topic of race had never been broached in our house. I instantly believed my parents were being racist. I never considered they might have had other issues with him.

I don't remember how we worked it out. I went out with Willie again, but although he was a very kind, gentle man who really wanted a relationship with me, I declined. To this day, I don't know if my parents were more upset about Willie's race than the fact he was that much older than me and a long distance truck driver. I think I decided against a relationship with Willie for those exact reasons.

Ten years later, when I told my mother I was dating a man named Tony (this was following a relationship with my first true boyfriend, a young Korean American man from the same karate school I attended, and an on-off relationship with a black man (who was not exactly marriage material and wore a three-quarter-length coat and platform shoes), her eyes lit up and she asked, "Is he Italian?" She seemed a bit bummed when I told her that, "No, he's Jamaican." But, again, was it racism or realism that had her concerned over an interracial relationship?

The only objection I ever did hear came from my uncle, who stated exactly what Spencer Tracy said to his daughter in *Guess Who's Coming to Dinner?* He wanted to know if I had considered the hardship our biracial children might face. Again, racism or realism? I will side with realism because my marriage was celebrated by all relatives, and my children were welcomed into the family without reservations. Even my adopted black son, Jeremy, who came to us at age five, was welcomed with the same open arms. To this day, one of my favorite memories is my father ushering his three grandchildren into a restaurant ahead of me, proud as all get out to be their grandfather.

I don't think we need to give you readers an entire history of race and race relations in America; you would have to have either never gone to school, never read a book, or never ventured outside of your house to not have a basic idea of how things went down. But the question is: when did things that were starting to get better do a U-turn and start going downhill?

No one questions that keeping a whole group of people as slaves, especially a group determined by the color of their skin, is a bad thing. No one questions that when a whole group of innocent persons are released into society as a freed people, they are going to be far behind those in society who were never slaves. No one questions that years of discrimination against people who were not white kept those people from attaining their dreams and a better life. In no way do we believe that freeing black slaves, fighting for racial equality, and eliminating discriminatory laws weren't the right things to do.

But why has our trajectory toward the elimination of racial discrimination taken an unpleasant downhill slide? Do people even realize it has? What the Left would like everyone to think is that nothing ever actually improved in this country and that white people are as racist against people of color as ever. We are told the racism of the past never went away; it just was disguised in many other forms, and now, we are bringing it out into the open, and white people should finally admit they have never stopped oppressing other races.

Here is a quick history lesson. Slavery was racist (racism being defined as discriminating and treating people badly simply because of the color of their skin) and bad. The civil rights movement was racialism (recognizing people who have a particular color of skin may have some issues in common: physical attributes, diseases, history, experiences, subcultures, maltreatment, and so on) and good. Why? Because there was an acceptance by many people of all colors that people of darker skin, mostly descendants of Africans (and, yes, slaves), had been, as a group, treated unfairly. It was obvious that race was a factor in the poor treatment of this group, and so work was done to change racist laws and make sure all citizens, including those in this particular racial group, had the right to have a life and liberty and to pursue happiness, as stated in the Declaration of Independence.

Then a new sort of racialism cropped up. This was the time of the Black Power movement and a pride in being black: Black is beautiful, afros, *Essence* magazine, and the rise of the black music industry with soul and R&B. In a sense, this was less of a separatist movement (although some of it was) and more of a "we are no longer going to feel ashamed of who we are." It was racialism by the group who had suffered racism. I think it was a necessary outgrowth of years of oppression, like a child becoming an adult, leaving the house, and making one's own name and life.

Over the next two decades, people of color made major inroads into much of the previously white-controlled arenas: business, politics, education, sports, music, film, and television. Maybe not as far as some people of color may have liked, but, realistically, when a group is less than 15 percent of the entire population of the country, that group is always likely to be less noticeably represented.[2] If you drive around India, you don't see white people on all the billboards, and if you watch a Bollywood movie (Hindi movies from the film capital, Bombay/Mumbai), you only see white people when they are doing a historical movie about British rule or when the movie is about Indians living in the United States or Canada. But there *are* white people living in India; they just are in a very small minority. Likewise, in Jamaica, whites have lived there a long time, but if you watch a Jamaican movie, you are going to see a majority black film.

During this time, as the twentieth century ended and the twenty-first century began, it seemed that this particular racialism was beginning to dwindle. It wasn't that black people were losing pride; it is just that the races and various subcultures were getting along better, people of different races were intermarrying, cultures and music and food were being shared and fused, having a black or Indian doctor was no big deal to whites, and blacks were enjoying country music and becoming country music stars. Being just American seemed to be a hit! We might recognize someone is of another race or a mix of races,

2.   United States Census Bureau. "Quick Facts." Accessed July 17, 2020. https://www.census.gov/quickfacts/fact/table/US/PST045219.

but it was in a good way—as in one loved what that partic-ular influence, race, or culture contributed to the positive vibe of society. Race recognition was acceptance and appreciation of all races. Even Black History Month, something one might call racialist, was really, when it was introduced, learning about nonwhite Americans of the past who had been overlooked in mainstream history, cheering their contributions and being happy that group of people were part of our country.

And then the Obama era hit and all racial progress seemed to come crashing to a halt. The Trayvon Martin incident and Black Lives Matter revved up what seemed to many a new racialism. But it quickly became obvious this was actually a new racism, a racism against whites and, to some extent, against foreign-born citizens, regardless of their skin tone being brown or black. While it may have appeared at the start that Black Lives Matter was for all people of color, over time it became evident that some were more equal than others as a recent CNN article exemplifies as it excoriated Indian-Americans for:

> …brown complicity in White supremacy, brown silence, brown fragility and the continuation of the model minority myth… and the need to… check their brown privilege.[3]

DAVE

I often wonder why I have divergent viewpoints with most other people of color in this country. And there are many reasons, but one in particular stands out. I recall one line

---

3. Dewan, Angela. "Indians are being held up as a model minority. That's not helping the Black Lives Matter movement." CNN. Last modified June 29, 2020. https://www.cnn.com/2020/06/29/world/indians-migrant-minority-black-lives-matter-intl/index.html.

from the movie *Guess Who's Coming to Dinner* (a classic and groundbreaker). While in heated discussion with his father concerning his relationship with his white fiancée, Dr. Prentice (played by Sidney Poitier) said, "Dad, you see yourself as a black man. I just see myself as a man." What did he mean by this? Simply put, he did not want his skin color to define him or control the trajectory of his life, an option not afforded his father, who grew up and lived through much more difficult times. And it really was an extraordinary gift he gave his son: the opportunity to pursue his life's passion of medicine, attend the finest schools, and enjoy something of a charmed life—a near impossibility just decades ago. But had his father gotten his way, his life would have had a shadow cast over it. His skin color would not have been just an "issue of pigmentation," as the white fiancée's father called it, but an outward expression of one's inner being, an armor put on to confront the hostile world that will inevitably lash out at you. It sometimes seems like being black and proud is akin to a simmering cauldron that can be turned up and sent boiling over at a moment's notice.

There was a time when this was a necessity. Walking down the wrong street or through the wrong neighborhood in the Jim Crow South could be dangerous if one wasn't aware of his or her own skin color. These lessons and subconscious feelings were passed down from father to son and mother to daughter, and as we inevitably find out, despite our every effort, in the end, we are much more like our parents than we may want to be. Without even trying, our mentality is passed down to our children, and then our grandchildren, generation after generation.

Perhaps this is where my own experience is different than most black Americans. My black father wasn't born in the United States, my black grandparents didn't live through the

Jim Crow era, and when they, through luck and hard work, were able to immigrate to Washington, DC, in 1974, it was long after the civil rights movement. My father, already a teenager, had a life of hardships living in Jamaica, but not because of his race. Growing up poor and in the mountains of Jamaica, the oldest of six, he was put to work at a young age. The stories of his childhood were not about drinking from certain water fountains or being harassed by the police; they were of long, arduous walks barefoot up and down the rocky unpaved mountain roads and of tending to the goats and chickens that would inevitably have to be slaughtered. Life was tough, and one had to work hard. That was the mentality he had growing up, and it was that mentality that helped him avoid the pitfalls of life as a black man in urban America. Life did get better when he came to the US, but the hard work never stopped. Even while attending high school, he worked a full-time job. While so many of his friends were heading to the corners, he was heading to work with his mother; they were employed as janitors cleaning office buildings. Sad to say, decades removed, many of those same friends are dead or in jail. I often wonder what his life might have been like if he hadn't been lucky enough to have been born poor in Jamaica.

If that proud black man is the simmering cauldron, I guess I'm a cold bucket of water. I am guilty of apathy in a time of increasing racial tensions, real or perceived. I'm still trying to figure out how the hell we got here. Growing up in the '90s, life was good. I never thought about race. I had white friends, black friends, Latino friends.... Race was never discussed or even thought much of. And then we had 9/11; we came together as Americans to fight a common enemy, Al-Qaeda and global terrorism. After almost eight years of war, the economy collapsed, and out of the US Senate, a new hope for the country arose. This was a turning point for America. *Hope and Change,* our first African American president! And things did change for the better, or at least they seemed to at first. Then, a young black teen was shot in Florida by a "white" Hispanic. Later, another black teen was shot attacking a police officer in Ferguson, and then a black drug dealer broke his neck riding in police van in Baltimore. FULL STOP. Racism is back! How exhausting....

It wasn't just racial tensions that had been stoked anew, but also a disintegration of the pride we used to have in being Americans. Now it seems we are global citizens. National borders are nothing more than political lines enforced by bigots and xenophobes. We should have been clued in when then presidential candidate Barack Obama chose Germany as a location to give a political speech. He didn't just view himself as an American hoping to lead the American people but as a Pied Piper whose leadership would be for all on earth. US policy wouldn't just be in interest of the American people, but rather it would be shaped with a global perspective.

This loss of pride in Americanism and becoming American for those who arrive at our shores has more damaging consequences than one might think. So much of one's ability to navigate through life is dependent on language and an understanding of culture and customs. Yet we are directly or indirectly encouraging people to not make that effort. Press 1 for English, press 2 for Spanish is fine; some people may be in process of learning English. It shouldn't, however, have been an avenue to avoid ever having to speak English at all, and, yet, that is what it has become. Even to encourage someone to improve their English-speaking skills can lead to accusations of xenophobia or a distaste for other languages. During my time working in construction, I have managed many workers who do not speak English, yet many of those laborers had the hope of one day finding a more comfortable job. I encouraged them to improve their English-speaking skills, but month after month and year after year, there was little change. The US has evolved in such a way that one can live in large cities without the need to be an English speaker. Certainly, this initially makes life easier for new arrivals, but in the long run, this convenience ends up being an obstacle to achieving success in America.

This striving for Americanism reminds me of a friend I made while living in Mexico. Only eighteen years old, I traveled to central Mexico to study Spanish in the mountain town of Guanajuato. It was a fantastic experience, although admittedly, I didn't learn as much Spanish as I could have. With the local university only blocks from my apartment and the drinking age being only eighteen, I spent most nights partying, often making my way home after sunrise. My friend, who I met at the language school I was attending, was twenty-five and had been accepted into law school. He wanted to learn Spanish so he could eventually work as an immigration attorney helping Central Americans come to the States. The irony was he was born in California to Mexican parents, yet here he was in Guanajuato learning Spanish. Of course, the obvious question was, why didn't he learn Spanish from his parents? The answer: they refused to teach him! They were so preoccupied with making sure that their son was an American first, they were worried that speaking Spanish at home would divide him between two cultures. Were their fears a bit overblown? Perhaps, but their intent was noble. They wanted their son to be completely accepted as an American, and in this end, they were successful. When I met him, I only saw a slightly obnoxious northern Californian with that laid-back Cali attitude.

He was an American, no hyphen.

PAT

Isn't that the way it should be? Americans—maybe of different hues and subcultures—but Americans? Shouldn't we be further along than we were in the year 2009 when, finally, a not-totally-white man became president? A man with a very white mother and a very dark African father? And, yet, in 2017 came a movie by Jordan Peale, *Get Out*, that showed just how those eight years of his presidency took us toward a new racist world. What some people (liberals) are claiming is just "racialism" is hardly that. It isn't just a movie about black subculture; it is a racist fantasy with whites as the boogeymen.

Let me explain. Recognizing someone is of a particular race is not racism, nor is it even racialism. I might use race in a physical description, but that is not racialism; it is an identifier. But it is racialism when I comment that someone is Indian when discussing a wedding because the difference between an American wedding celebration and an Indian wedding celebration is about three days! It is a time factor issue! I might mention race as a group, white or black, if the issue is cultural and the participation is an event with an entire group of people from a particular race (and usually associated also with location, education, religion, and professions) so that someone might adapt to the circumstances. If I tell someone we are going to visit a Muslim family dinner at home, it might be a warning to be sure one is more clothed upon arrival or not to bring BBQ pork ribs along to share. It is not racist to make these distinctions. It is racialism but not racism to point out a quality in a particular group of people unless one is making an unfair across-the-board assumption (almost always negative) about an entire race of people. *Then* it turns into racism.

Get Out, a Jordan Peele film people have called the 2017 update of *Guess Who's Coming to Dinner*, is considered only a racialist film by the Left who believe that the depiction of whites is true and fair, but what a mind-blowing claim this is. I won't get into a criticism of the horror aspects of the movie or the acting ability of the actors and actresses, but while *Guess Who's Coming to Dinner* allowed us to consider if we are dealing with a latent racism in ourselves or the reality of a world wherein interracial relationships were still illegal in seventeen states, *Get Out* is a film warning blacks that whites should not be trusted in any way, shape, or form, and to *Get Out* of *any* relationship with white people because they will end up destroying you. And this film came out more than fifty years after the Civil Rights Act of 1964! How did we go so far backwards in thinking?

Lest you think I am exaggerating, let me run through this film (warning: spoilers ahead) and the rampant racism exhibited here.

The film starts with a bizarre scene of a black man accidentally lost in the suburbs. I guess he is supposed to be feeling what a white person might feel if they were stranded in a black area of the city: scared and threatened. So, this black man is freaking out while walking in this lovely neighborhood that he must be thinking is 100 percent white because, um…black people don't live in the suburbs in 2017 and it is dangerous for blacks to be walking about?

Let me back up to 1982 when my black husband and I moved to Berwyn Heights, Maryland, an all-white town, barring one woman and my husband. He went jogging one day and some fellow driving by told him to get out of the neighborhood. He yelled back, "Sorry, I can't because I live here!" No question, he found that rather upsetting, but that was an isolated incident, and he never had another problem in the next thirty years. Certainly, he wasn't really thinking he would be assaulted or shot for being in a white neighborhood. Of course, in 2020, there was a story that was to become the new version of the Trayvon Martin story: a black man goes jogging, and three white men hunt him down and shoot him dead. The press made it seem that the motive of the white men was purely to murder an innocent black man. What really appeared to have occurred was three men decided to police their neighborhood rather than let law enforcement do it, perhaps because law enforcement was not doing much about it. They believed Arbery to be a thief who had committed some recent crimes (although they did not have proof of this) and when they saw Arbery coming from a dwelling that was under construction, they assumed he was up to no good, chased him down with their truck, confronted him with a shotgun, and attempted to make a citizen's arrest. The story is a bit confusing at this point and we need to wait for all the evidence to be presented in court and see if that evidence supports homicide by these three men; however, it should be noted: unless one's life is threatened or that of another, attempting a citizen's arrest using a weapon for a petty crime that is unproven is unacceptable.

But, the problem with the media story was that this was immediately presented as a hate crime and that twenty-five-year-old Ahmaud Arbery was absolutely jogging innocently around the neighborhood. That this may not be what happened was ignored by the media because they had their new racist white people story. On the contrary, the evidence suggests

Ahmaud Arbery was not jogging but was trespassing on private property. What his intention was as to why he entered the uninhabited dwelling that was under construction, we can only speculate. The fact Arbery had once brought a gun to a school event, was arrested for stealing a flat-screen television from a store, was found parked far off the road in an area known for drug dealing, looked and behaved like a thug when the police questioned him. None of this was publicized by the media, who repeatedly published a high school graduation photo of Arbery in a suit. "Black While Jogging" became the new "Hands Up, Don't Shoot." The message the media propagated is that white people are to be feared by blacks even during the most mundane activities of life. . This was the message of *Get Out*, and it resonated in this new world of "Black while _____ (fill in the blank with any verb)."

Fast-forward to 2015. I am living in Bowie, Maryland, and my cat goes missing. I make up fliers and take them around the neighborhood, placing them in mailboxes. I go into a fancy home cul-de-sac, and a black woman in a Mercedes SUV pulls up to me and asks what I am doing in the neighborhood! I had to laugh. I was a white woman (and I kind of looked like crap that day) wandering around in a fancy all-black neighborhood. I told her something along the lines of what my husband had said some forty years ago, that "I live here" and that "my cat is missing." I certainly understood why she questioned why I was there; I never thought I was physically in danger walking around in that nice neighborhood.

So, back to *Get Out*. Suddenly, a car pulls up, and a white man (at least we are supposed to believe it is) hits the guy over the head, stuffs him in the trunk, and drives away. Would you call this a rather racist depiction? I am sure if a white guy had been walking around in a nice black neighborhood and been attacked and carted away, black viewers would not have been pleased with that scene.

But it gets far worse. Professional black guy is dating white girl in the city, and they are a happy couple. All good. Then, she invites him home to meet her parents. As soon as the couple drives into the wooded countryside, black guy freaks out! Cue ominous music. He is going into white people country! Then, sure enough, they hit a deer, and the cop who comes to their aid asks for the black guy's license even though he wasn't driving. Is this *Macon County Line*? Anyhoo, they get to the white girl's house where her well-educated liberal parents welcome him with hugs and proceed to say every clichéd racialist statement one can think of, as do their white friends ("I voted for Obama," "I like Tiger Woods," and so on). Then, the racist horror story follows.

Black guy finds out that all the white people just want black bodies to use for their dying white relatives and themselves, so they can continue on in those strapping physiques and delicious brown skins (I know, it makes zero sense at all, except that, I guess, white folks really don't like being white because white is ugly and racist and stupid). Then, black guy finds out that he is *not* the only black guy his white girlfriend has dated; he finds a photo album of her with a dozen black guys. *Oh!* She *never* loved him! She is only a white siren luring black men to their deaths.

Whew! I'm exhausted. What the heck is this crap of a movie? White people bad. Black people good. Black people should never, ever be around white people because white people bad.

Is this not as racist as racist gets? Can you imagine if the original *Guess Who's Coming to Dinner* devolved into the black fiancé killing everyone in the house? Yet, *Get Out* was lauded by the Left as a great movie about race relations!

> A young black man meets his white girlfriend's parents in Jordan Peele's chilling satire of liberal racism in the US.[4]—Mark Kermode/The Guardian
>
> More than just a standard-issue thriller, this brutal, smart movie is impeccably made, as well as surprising, shocking, and funny, while also offering a compassionate, thoughtful look at race.[5]—Jeffrey M. Anderson/Common Sense Media

Okay, "a chilling satire of liberal racism" kind of makes me laugh because this is where the black Left turns on the white Left, those folks they claim they want as "allies," a role which forces whites to accept a subservient position, the exact reverse of the racism of the past. And it doesn't really matter how much one grovels; if you are white, you will always be racist. That's what this film points out. Satire it is *not*! It is the reality of the new racism in the leftist movement. It actually says to liberal whites, "Get out of the movement!"

Now, to the second review. Hahaha! The movie is a compassionate, thoughtful look at race? Wow! What movie was this guy watching? All I saw was hatred of white people, through and through. Regardless of which ending you prefer (there are two: the final one where a black hero saves the black boyfriend from being murdered by the white people and the original one where the white cops arrest the black boyfriend for murder

4.   Kermode, Mark. "Get Out review – tea, bingo… and racial terror." *The Guardian*. Last modified March 19, 2017. https://www.theguardian.com/film/2017/mar/19/get-out-review-jordan-peele-racism-america.

5.   Anderson, Jefferson M. "Get Out." Common Sense Media. Accessed July 7, 2020. https://www.commonsensemedia.org/movie-reviews/get-out.

of the white people and he gets life in prison), not one white person is a bit decent or a victim and not one black person is anything but good and all blacks are victims.

This is where we find ourselves in race relations in 2020. Regardless of the outcome of the 2020 elections, this mindset is still here, and we have to fight to get back to the dream of Martin Luther King that we should see each other as equals and brothers and sisters regardless of our color.

DAVE

Like anyone else, I enjoy plopping on the couch for hours binging Netflix. For the most part, it really is a great platform for a wide variety of shows. With so many series to pick from, how do I decide what to watch? First, it must pass the fifteen minutes test. I watch fifteen minutes, and if there is any overt racial pandering, I am done with it. I won't watch it. Perhaps I'm overly sensitive, but I don't think the producers of these shows really understand how nauseating it is to be spoon-fed feel-good race messages. Don't get me wrong, there are plenty of shows that focus on race in a constructive and cerebral way. Hollywood, to some extent, reflects the current struggles of society, and in a country with a deep racial history, it is inevitable that race issues will be dramatized and reflected upon in cinema. Unfortunately, the messaging has become simplistic, gratuitous, and nauseating. The new trend is to change the race of a well-known character (James Bond, for example). It's been rumored that Idris Elba is in contention to be the new Bond. I love Idris Elba, he was fantastic in *The Wire* and, according to the women in my life, a very handsome black man. The only problem is, James Bond is not a black guy. His background has been well-established by author Ian Fleming—he's half

Scottish, half Swiss. Idris Elba playing James Bond would be just as ridiculous as Sean Connery playing Shaft; however, in our current "woke" culture, entertainment media producers make these obnoxious decisions. Black people don't need James Bond, we have Nick Fury, Luke Cage, and Black Panther. Let James Bond be white.

Another obnoxious trend I've noticed is the portrayal of whites as being morally weaker characters. Look out for it in the next drama series you watch. It will usually be a middle-aged white man wearing a suit and tie who crumbles when faced with a tough ethical dilemma, only for a wise older black of meager means to come in and heroically make the right decision. Is it petty for me to notice these things? Perhaps. But it always makes me roll my eyes. To be clear, there is nothing wrong with strong, black, moral characters, but there is a thing called subtlety. Instead, Hollywood prefers to beat you over the head with the idea. Who do they think they are preaching to? Certainly not myself. Watch any award show to get the real answer. They are not seeking the approval of black people; they are seeking the approval of their rich, mostly white, self-righteous peers. Even those who are left-leaning find these shows to be embarrassing. They are contests in which each successive celebrity attempts to out-pander the next. To answer the question of who they are preaching to? Themselves!

But while Hollywood types are having their own private circle jerk, there are liberals who genuinely feel they have an obligation to address their "privilege" and reflect their understanding in how they interact with people of color. There is no malicious intent, but they ironically cater to stereotypes of the black experience. My experience, my father's experience, and even my brother's experience are not the same. A poor black kid from Compton, California, is not going to have the same outlook as a middle-class black from Chicago or Boston. Or in my case, the perspective you assume I have based on my skin color may not match up with what you were taught in a liberal arts class on black history. Even if the intent is to convey understanding, expressions of white guilt toward blacks isn't compassionate or caring; it's quite obnoxious. This doesn't just apply to race issues, either. It applies to all areas of life. I'm relatively tall at six foot one—not so tall as to stand out but tall enough where no one would ever consider me to be short. I can tell you from my own experience with short friends of mine, it can be tough being a five-foot-six guy.

There are a couple of ways I've seen it handled. Either they are completely comfortable with it, and they never allow it to define them or become the focus of their life. Or it can go the complete opposite way. We've met him, the guy with a Napoleon complex who walks around like a peacock looking for a reason to be offended. I've listened as they waxed on about the lack of respect they receive, how bigger guys go out of their way to bump them while walking across the bar. Every slight, they feel, is due to their height—and since that is what they are hyper-focused on, it is. But who do you think lives a better life: the guy who accepts it or the guy who dwells on it? Do you think it does me any good to pat my buddy on the back to tell him, "Sorry that you're short, but let me tell you, being tall is way overrated"? What do you think his response will be? Nothing I can write here. Whether it's race, height, or sex, we can be aware of how our differences impact each of us differently, but we should stop short of groveling. It's not productive and is embarrassing to everyone.

There was a time when I can understand why a dislike of whites may have been pushed. In the late '60s or when we were only a few years from the civil rights movement, one can understand that blacks were certainly still feeling the sting of blatant discrimination by whites. But in 2020, I question the motive. Not only do we still have hatred being pushed, it's given rise to supremacy movements by people of color. Make no mistake about it, Black Lives Matter promotes separatism, and in moments of candor, their members profess racial supremacy. They seek not equality but the subjugation of other races, particularly the white race. As a person of color, I'm genuinely perplexed that so many white liberals go along with this thinking, and at what point do they become insulted? Without the support of white people, we would not have had a Civil Rights Act in 1968. We would not have had laws protecting minorities in the workplace. Let us not forget that 600,000 Americans died in the Civil War, more than WWI and WWII combined. When we look back through history, every group of people face hardships, wars, famines, enslavement, and genocide. While I could bemoan my own situation being born black in America in the 1980s, what of my white Jewish grandfather who fled Nazi Germany in the 1930s to avoid Hitler's rising oppression of the Jews? Can I honestly say my life at any time was as difficult? By the grace of God and the foresight of my great-grandparents, they saw where the country was heading and left in the nick of time. They came to America where they were able to pursue life, liberty, and happiness.

As someone who is mixed-race, this new antagonism has put me and continues to put me in an awkward position. I remember lifting weights back in the day at my local gym. We were a fairly tight-knit group of guys from all walks of life and had been working out together for years. One of those guys I worked out with we called Roach. We all had nicknames in the gym. There was 50 (he liked 50 Cent), Tebow (he looked like Tebow), and guess why they called me Tiger? Well, Roach always did more talking than he did lifting, and on this occasion, he was expressing concern about a situation at work. He had spent the last several days riding around with his boss's daughter, his boss's white daughter. (Roach was a big black guy.) It made him nervous—not because she was the boss's daughter but because she was white. She even smelled weird! Yes, he asked me if I had noticed that, too, that white women smell funny. Well, there are times when you contribute to the conversation and other times when you just shake your head feigning understanding. Did this guy not realize why my hair (this was a time I still had it) was straight and not curled? And that I wasn't as dark as some of the other guys in the gym? Well, as far as white women smelling a certain way, maybe I never noticed because my own mother was white. This sort of scenario has popped up several times in my life. Here I am, a person of white heritage, having a conversation with another black person who is disparaging whites.

For those of us people of color with white parents and grandparents, how do we fit in this new world? As mentioned before, instead of the colorblind society we should have, we are regressing to a world where all we see is color, where whites are the enemy and blacks need safe spaces. No one has been able to explain what I'm supposed to do. I watch a movie like *Get Out* that is a box-office hit. A black man is taken to the burbs by his evil white girlfriend and her family to be lobotomized and have his body snatched. It wasn't just a horror movie, but a warning to black people to avoid white society.

When I watch that movie, I don't see evil white people; I see my aunts and uncles, grandparents, and cousins. How do I *Get Out* from my own heritage? Maybe I ought to ask Colin Kaepernick. A biracial man raised in the suburbs by two white parents who joined up with Black Lives Matter (BLM) and created a movement of kneeling down for black oppression he never felt. Only in easy times like these can a multi-millionaire find an excuse to nail himself to a cross. Is there any other place and time in the history of man that is better than here and now? No, and he's proof.

CHAPTER THREE

GREEN BOOK

THE PSYCHOLOGICAL RACE WAR
AGAINST WHITE PEOPLE

"The Negro needs the white man to free him from his fears. The white man needs the Negro to free him from his guilt."

MARTIN LUTHER KING, JR.[1]

DAVE

Let's imagine it is 1999. A movie comes out about segregation in the Deep South. The audience is taken on a ride with two protagonists as they wind their way through the Southern states, where violence and racism were the norm and segregation was legal. Viewers are introduced to the Negro Motorist Green Book, something probably few whites or even blacks today are familiar with. It is a lodging and eatery guide for POC of the time where blacks could find hotels and restaurants that would allow nonwhites to stay and to dine, legally and safely. It is a two-hour look at life for blacks in the South before the Civil Rights Act of 1964.

---

1.   Hughes, Coleman. "Martin Luther King, Colorblind Radical." *WSJ Opinion*. Last modified January 17, 2019. https://www.wsj.com/articles/martin-luther-king-colorblind-radical-11547769741.

One would think this movie would be popular with the black community. The movie features a wealthy and educated black pianist with an upper-class upbringing. His counterpart, however, who works as his bodyguard/driver, is a lower-class white guy with a somewhat seedy disposition. During their travels, their unique arrangement allows the white man to see the plight of black Americans in a different light. He better appreciates the many hardships endured by blacks in the segregated South and gains a newfound respect for POC. His enlightenment isn't his solely but is also shared by the black pianist who realizes that racist views held by many whites are not engrained in their souls. Through their shared experience and personal interactions, he realizes that people can change and that their prejudices can be lessened. The movie concludes with the white driver's family inviting the black man into their home. And to top it off, the black character is gay and the movie incorporates LGBT issues! It's a fabulous script with great acting. This movie is a shoo-in for the Academy Award for Best Picture. If it had won the award twenty years ago, the film would have been touted as a huge win for African Americans, as it starred a black actor and dealt with racism in America.

But, no, this movie won the Academy Award in 2019, and the black community—at least the vocal left-leaning side—were incensed that this movie got such high accolades. Why were they so enraged? Because white people left the movie feeling happy? Yes, happy! An unacceptable outcome! If a movie about racism doesn't make white people leave with a sense of self-loathing, it is a failure and an insult to blacks in America.

Which leads us to the new concept of "White fragility, a state in which even a minimum amount of racial stress becomes intolerable...."[2] In other words, whites can't handle learning about their involvement and support of racism in America. Spike Lee's *BlacKkKlansman* would have forced whites to face white supremacism in our country and their role in it, and that would make whites feel bad. Therefore, the Academy wouldn't dare give Lee's film the award for Best Picture. *Green Book*, on the other hand, certain critics say is just another "white savior" movie, another *Driving Miss Daisy*, where the white hero helps the suffering black man feel better about himself and, in turn, makes white viewers feel better about themselves as well.

Is this really how African Americans and their "allies" see black and white people, or is this just the Left suffering from black leftist fragility and white leftist fragility? Are they unable to have a view on anything without always seeing a white racist lurking in the background? Is nothing good ever good enough? Is anything good not ever really good? Is what the Left really telling us all is that our country is hopeless when it comes to race? It does seem that way. Nothing one does, says, or puts into law will ever be good enough. Like an abusive relationship, the offender will always come back with harder blows because the person they are victimizing can never do enough to please him.

PAT

When I watched *Green Book*, a strange feeling came over me at the end. I felt pride in being white, *and* I felt black pride as well! How is that, you ask? Well, both those feelings in myself— pride at being who I am as a white person and pride in people of different-colored skin who had struggled to survive under difficult conditions and make something of themselves.

---

2.   DiAngelo, Robin. *White Fragility*. Boston: Beacon Press, 2018. p. 51.

I can look back to when my children were young and I was homeschooling them. Because traditional history textbooks were a bit lacking in including the achievements worldwide of people who were not white (as they also lacked the achievements of women), I made sure to include in my curriculum stories of black people and other people of color who had contributed to our world, especially to our country. I felt pride in those people, and I wanted my children to feel that pride as well. I didn't dis white people in doing so. I also presented histories of great white people (and, yes, that includes great white men) because they also were contributors to achievements in freedom, science, and the arts. And, after all, my children had white grandparents and aunts and uncles and ancestors. I wanted them to feel proud to be connected to whites as well as blacks and all the other colors in the world, for that matter. We had Chinese renters in our house, mostly students from Beijing, so I taught my children some of the fine contributions of the Chinese culture as well. This didn't mean I overlooked bad things that people or governments have done in history (I understand, for example, that the Communist government and the Wuhan virus—yes, the COVID-19 virus that seems to have come from Wuhan—are not identical to Chinese citizens of that country). I made sure my children didn't equate a race of people with bad or good. I wanted my children to feel pride in the human race, not just the race society labeled them.

Fast-forward to the decade of Obama and onward. White man bad. Black man good. If you as a white or black person don't agree with "white man bad" and "black man good," regardless of the topic, matter, or circumstances, you are a white supremacist. And because of this change of attitude, I started finding myself becoming defensive about being white and starting to dislike new movies and books that included stories about discrimination against people of color or about the history of people of color because within those films and books was the new message, "white man bad, black man good." If one is white, one *must* feel bad about being white and about all whites in history, and if one is black, one must hate whites and all whites in history. Even Black History Month has become infected by Black Lives Matter and the guilt white people should feel. The program is no longer about great black men and women of the United States in history but about all the bad things white people have done to black people in the past and how white people must compensate for all the misery they have caused (along with a Marxist agenda, as we will discuss later). I am not sure what my grandchildren should feel sitting in a class that says "all white people bad, all black people good" when they are mixed-race and part of a family of all races.

Not only must one hate the white race for their historical behavior, it is now being pushed that white people are genetically damaged.

This is what actor and show host Nick Cannon (ex-husband to singer Mariah Carey) had to offer on a radio show:

> When you'd have a person that has the lack of pigment, the lack of melanin, that they know that they will be annihilated. So therefore, however they got the power, they have the lack of compassion that … Melanin comes with compassion. Melanin comes with soul that we call … We call it. We're soul brothers and sisters. That's the melanin that connects us. So the people that don't have it are a little … and I 'm going to say this carefully … are a little less. And where the term actually comes from, because I'm bringing it all the way back around to

Minister Farrakhan, to where they may not have them compassion or when they were sent to the Mountains of Caucuses, when they didn't have the power of the sun, that was the sun then started to deteriorate them.

So then they're acting out of fear. They're acting out of low self-esteem. They're acting out of a deficiency. So, therefore the only way that they can act is evil. The only way they can ... they have to rob, steal, rape, kill, and fight ... in order to survive.

So then these people who didn't have what we had ... and when I say we, I speak of the melanated people ... They had to be savages. They had to be barbaric because they're in these Nordic mountains. They're in these rough torrential environments. So they're acting as animals.

So they're the ones that are actually closer to animals. They're the ones that are actually the true savages.[3]

What is most frightening about this Nick Cannon rant is not how bizarre his thinking is but that a great number of black Americans cheered what he had to say, cheered a set of beliefs just as awful as those of white eugenicists prior to World War II who claimed blacks were inferior, defective, or degenerate.[4]

Not only does this new view of the white race need to be flooded across the nation via the media and colleges, one needs to start in the public schools as young as kindergarten to make very sure the indoctrination takes.

3.   "Nick Cannon Transcript: Fired by ViacomCBS for 'Hateful Speech.'" Rev. Interview Transcripts. Last modified July 14, 2020. https://www.rev.com/blog/transcripts/nick-cannon-transcript-fired-by-viacomcbs-for-perpetuating-anti-semitism.
4.   Eugenics in the United States." Wikipedia. Last modified August 13, 2020. https://en.wikipedia.org/wiki/Eugenics_in_the_United_States.

White guilt and the requiring of white guilt is nothing but a new form of racism. *Green Book* had the audacity to return to the former positive melding of black and white pride, and this brave, new world was not going to allow that to happen.

So, what on earth could cause a return to the Black Power of the '60s and '70s hostility toward life in America and a need to inspire antagonism toward white people, even requiring white people to turn on themselves after all the progress that was made during the last half decade in race relations? Why the new white guilt?

I believe it has to do with the Left losing ground in the political realm as identity politics was dwindling; after all, their power lies in that exact formula: separating groups of people in spite of claiming, "We are the people."

When *Green Book* won Best Picture at the Oscars in 2019, Spike Lee walked out of the room in anger. His *BlacKkKlansman* also had been nominated for best picture. I hadn't seen it, but I viewed *Do the Right Thing* and *Jungle Fever* back in 1989 and 1991 when they were in the theaters. And I remember what I thought about them at the time: Spike Lee never got his head out of the '70s when he was a teen! It was as though he was stuck in time while the rest of society had moved on. The films reminded me of a place on the border of South Carolina and Georgia that I decided to check out as I was driving to Florida. A sign on the side of the road beckoned us, "Authentic African Village." In South Carolina? Now, I had been to West Africa and had stayed in a truly authentic African village, a place called Tchitchou in the north of Togo, so, damn, I had to see this!

I drove to the entrance and parked. I entered the Oyotunji Yoruba African Kingdom, an intentional village started in 1970 by some back-to-Africa fellows who never made it back to

Africa. The place was freaky. It was like some weird rundown, bizarre campsite with large cement statues for worshipping idols, like the God of Metal, which had wrenches and knives and a gun at the altar. I smelled weed and saw some disheveled people sitting about. There was going to be some voodoo ceremony of sorts on another evening of the week. As I was leaving (as quick as I could following the short tour I politely endured), I saw a busload of ladies from a local black Baptist church arriving. I think they were going to be a wee surprised at what they were about to see. There was nothing authentic about the "village," and it was pretty much some black hippie commune appropriating African culture, a culture these American blacks had no real concept of. They have a nice website now, so maybe they have become more authentic over the years. But when I visited, about the time Spike Lee's film came out, it appeared to be some dropouts of 1970s society who didn't have the money to buy a ticket to Benin because they were too stoned to work. I will say, though, that the guide was very nice to me, so they did have their heart in whatever this place was.

It just seemed so out of sync with the times, and this is what I felt was wrong with Spike Lee's films. It was as if he didn't like how things were moving forward racially, so he had to throw a keg of dynamite into society to try to wreck progress.

Spike Lee was clearly not in favor of interracial relationships or having anything to do with white people. Like some of the Black Power movements of the '60s and '70s, he did not encourage the mixing of races but rather separatism. I think, at the time, I found the movies interesting but shook my head and relegated them to the far-left wing of political and societal thinking. And life went on without much impact from Spike Lee and his philosophy of race relations.

But after *Green Book* came out some almost thirty years later and Lee threw his shitfit at the Oscars, I thought I needed to restudy his films to see if I was off base about their impact back in the '90s. I decided I would have a Spike Lee movie day and view all three of these films in chronological order. I found it a fascinating and enlightening journey. I'll take you readers along with me.

Do the Right Thing came out in 1989. It was about a blazing hot day in a poor black Brooklyn neighborhood, and racial tension was simmering in the hearts of the people there—black, white, and Korean. I expected it would be a "hate Whitey" movie as Spike Lee tends toward representing white people as the only truly racist people and not much else. I was actually quite surprised by the movie. I liked it. I not only liked it; I thought it was quite brilliant, engaging, and hopeful. How the heck was this a Spike Lee Joint? I was confused.

Do the Right Thing actually shows the blacks of the neighborhood as quite racist and racially aggressive themselves. They are disrespectful toward the Koreans who run the liquor store, threaten a white man who has moved into the neighborhood, and harass an Italian pizza shop owner who has been serving the community for twenty-five years. The white Italians and the Koreans are really quite kind toward the residents and make all efforts to get along. A couple of young black guys get upset that the pizza shop owner, Sal, doesn't have blacks among the photos of famous people on his wall or permit them to come in with a blaring boom box playing rap. The movie ends with a riot, the shop burns down, but Sal forgives one of the instigators, who actually worked for him, and pays him his wages owed.

Wow. Not all white people are bad. Black people can act racist and unkindly. Some black people who reviewed the movie were seriously upset with the depiction of the blacks in the neighborhood. Funny, though, my mother-in-law's all-black neighborhood had similar attitudes toward businesses owned by nonblacks and with whites in general. True, this was back in the 1970s, but the attitude did exist. So, why did Spike Lee make a movie acknowledging that blacks could act racist and whites could behave well that had a hopeful ending like *West Side Story*? Certainly, I know why historically blacks feel discriminated against (and the movie alluded to this and this was fine), and we know why some of the anger is even justified. But we also know that anger needs to be ameliorated and folks need to understand each other and work to get along, that *both* sides need to do so (there was one older black man in the movie who was the voice of reason for the neighborhood along with Sal, the Italian). Nice. The movie was actually nice.

However, maybe I read the ending wrong. Some write that it wasn't a hopeful ending at all. They say that Sal and Mookie (the black employee that he paid) just came to a mutual acceptance of the way things were, that this was just another day in the hood, and that, in spite of the civil rights movement, blacks were still not able to win the fight against white supremacy. Oh, well, maybe, then, it is a normal Spike Lee film.

But I did find it odd that the movie *still* felt like the early '70s and not the end of the '80s. Why was the movie twenty years behind the times? Sure, maybe there were pockets of seething racism in the '80s and '90s, but, in general, the country had come quite far from that kind of thinking over the two decades after the civil rights movement and the Black Power movement. But, isn't that just it? White supremacy hasn't been vanquished, or so we are being told.

Then, I watched *Jungle Fever*, and oh my God! The subtlety of *Do the Right Thing* was totally gone. The movie came out just two years later, and it was nothing but vicious anger by whites toward blacks and vice versa. A black man has an affair with a white woman (he's married, she's not), and all hell breaks loose. The man's wife throws him out (justified), but her hatred toward white women (not just the mistress) is extreme. Then, the white woman's brothers beat the crap out of their sister. Dad even gets in a few blows. Later, the black man becomes the white woman's boyfriend and takes her to his home where his preacher father says the most repulsive things to her about being a Jezebel white women who sleeps with black men to make up for all the white slave-owner wives who really wanted dark meat during the plantation days. It was disgusting. It was anti-Christian and anti-white.

The woman should have dumped her immoral, stupid boyfriend for bringing her into such a situation. But, no, a few minutes later, they are playacting a fight on the street, and when he has her pinned to the hood of the car, the police show up and (gasp) think he is assaulting her. The movie just gets stupider when the conclusion is made that the only reason whites and blacks have sex is curiosity and any mixed-race children born of such relations are damned. Oh, and everyone uses every horrid racial slur I have ever heard and never heard. It was the '90s, for God's sake! I had been married to a black man for ten years and had three happy biracial and black kids, and the movie seemed like it was made before interracial marriage was legal. What world did Spike Lee live in?

Fast-forward to *BlacKkKlansman*. This movie actually does take place in the '70s. But even for that time, the movie seems to really overpaint white people as stupid redneck, black-hating, slur-spewing slime. I felt like I was beaten over the head for two hours. Oddly, the blacks of the Black Power movement (including Stokely Carmichael) were saying just as awful separatist things about whites. So it was a weird movie to watch because I think one version of blatant racism was supposed to be wrong and the other version of blatant racism was supposed to be right.

But *why*? Why is Spike Lee forever seemingly twenty to fifty years behind the times? Why does he want to push racial separation and hatred? My only answer is the one I think is true with the Left in general: they want the anger, agitation, and identity politics of the '60s and '70s to continue, even increase, and they have become frustrated that it was toning down. So, every so often, it is time to turn up the heat again, and what better way to do it than through film? When people watch movies and are told this is how things are, they often believe it. The Left needs to keep the pressure on, and along comes a movie like *Green Book* that preaches something different. How dare this happen! Bring on *BlacKkKlansman* and *Get Out*. Let's not forget about racism and white guilt and if you aren't willing to accept things are still really bad, it is because of white fragility.

White fragility, you say? What is that? Social Justice Professor Robin DiAngelo defines it as "the disbelieving defensiveness that white people exhibit when their ideals about race and racism are challenged – and particularly when they feel implicated in white supremacy."[5] She finds that fragility is being more upset with the mention of racism than the practice of it.

5.   Waldman, Katy. "A Sociologist Examines the 'White Fragility' That Prevents White Americans from Confronting Racism." *The New Yorker*. Last modified July 23, 2018. https://www.newyorker.com/books/page-turner/a-sociologist-examines-the-white-fragility-that-prevents-white-americans-from-confronting-racism?fbclid=IwAR3z6 E1K_Ts3UgvVt-NzJ9pT8UrSwlIiJ5MMUVYfdxxdKn7DNukHtYQryYM.

But then, that is the interesting conundrum the Left wants to encircle whites and more conservative blacks with. If one dares object to or gets tired of having white guilt shoved down one's throat, of racism by whites against people of color being brought up constantly and in instances when it may not be accurate, of going to a movie and having their whiteness or the whiteness of their relatives mocked and insulted throughout, and of having to grovel, well, then, one is suffering from white fragility (even if you are black).

And, there is no end to the abuse one is supposed to tolerate to be considered not a racist, not fragile, not uncaring about discrimination against people of color. Why, for only $2500, a white woman and nine of her friends can attend a dinner thrown by Regina Jackson, a black woman, and Sara Rao, an Indian American who is as viciously left and anti-white as anyone can be (check out her Twitter feed), where they will spend the evening suffering more degradation than an EST seminar of the 1970s. Before the dinner, they are required to read DiAngelos' *White Fragility* book. Then they must have their subconscious racism challenged. And by the end of dinner, they must surely confess to being racist scum of the earth. Oh, and white men and white female Trump supporters aren't invited because they are "lost causes," according to Rao and Jackson.[6] In my opinion, if you are a liberal white woman who pays to be pussy-whipped by these two racist twats, you deserve what you get.

But while this crazy dinner may be considered an outlier of bizarre leftist attention-getting, what of all those classes

6.   Cinone, Danielle, and Hannah Frishberg. "'WHITE FRAGILITY' White women are paying $2.5K for dinner to be told all the ways they're racist." *The Sun*. Last modified February 5, 2020. https://www.the-sun.com/news/358294/white-women-dinner-racist-race-paying/.

companies now force employees to take? What are they called? Diversity awareness training? I have never actually had to participate in one of these things, but the idea makes me want to throw up. Somehow the concept of sitting in a room where I am being told I somehow have failed to treat people of other races or cultures (or genders!) in a proper manner is rather insulting. I don't care to role-play how to behave. Furthermore, having looked through a number of PowerPoints for teaching diversity in the workplace, it comes across as a leftist, anti-white, anti-Christian, anti-conservatism bunch of brainwashing, especially if you are a member of the "dominant" (read: white) culture.

DAVE

This in part encapsulates the attitude white Leftists have toward minorities. On one hand, they claim to want equality, yet application of their ideology creates distance between ethnic groups, amplifies what makes us different, and invents new ways for us to feel apart. Blacks and white are equal, they say, and then they list in excruciating detail just how unlike themselves black people are, as if we lack a shared humanness, seemingly unaware of the insulting nature of their concern.

Liberal paternalism toward minorities has been a complaint of many black conservatives, or any conservative for that matter, for decades now. Looking back at our human history over that last several thousand years, suffering and hardship has been the norm. It was through these hardships, however, that we adapted and grew; the weak died and the strong survived. We have come to understand that struggle while in the moment an unappreciated burden molds our character, strengthens one's resolve, and nurtures our industrious nature. This is why the paternalistic liberal attitude is so dangerous for black Americans. Whether out of fear or guilt, white liberals holding those of color to a different standard lowers expectations, builds in an excuse for failure, and removes the impetuous to grow.

Perhaps the most egregious example of this is the pamphlet that was released by the National Museum of African American History and Culture.[7] This pamphlet, written by an older white woman described "whiteness," the traditions and attitudes that generally define white Americans. The context for listing these traits was to show how it would be unfair to project these values onto people of color. What kind of white cultural values and practices does this woman think doesn't apply to blacks? The nuclear family, rational linear thinking, individualism, work ethic, planning for the future, respecting authority...to name a number of these "white traits." But these values are not exclusively those of white people; they are values of people of all colors around the world. In an attempt to be a white "ally" to blacks Americans, this woman attributes to white people what amounts to the building blocks of any advanced society and implies that those values are not part of the African American community. Ironically, white supremacists would agree. This pamphlet is akin to the beliefs of Black Lives Matter, who reject the "Western prescribed nuclear family." Why are these organizations so hellbent on shepherding black people away from institutions and practices that bolster success and stability? And to think, they hold themselves up as the black man's best friend.

7. Staff. "How Is This 'White Culture' ONLY?!: Smithsonian Pamphlet Is Downright INSANE." Glenn Beck. Last modified July 16, 2020. https://www.glennbeck.com/blog/how-is-this-white-culture-only-smithsonian-pamphlet-is-downright-insane.

PAT

There is no doubt that our country has had a racist past and that discrimination has a long and damaging arm over people of color throughout the past decades. As a white woman, I am not ignorant of that. But I also will not live in the past, and I will not believe we cannot grow as a people over time through interaction and understanding. And by growing, I don't mean attending classes that tell us how we should think and how we should feel guilty. And if the Left does not think this can be achieved (even with all the force-feeding), then what even is the point of constantly badgering people to bring about white guilt? One can only believe that the end goal is for white people to retreat from all communion with people of color, to retreat from the school system and politics and business. It is the old Black Power wish that white people become extinct. Only problem is: with the number of white people in this country— they are still in the majority—white guilt and fragility may become the white rage the Left claims is really the cause of all the race problems we have. And that is how separatism and apartheid win out regardless of which race is on top.

So, has anything changed since the Spike Lee's films of the 1990 era and 2019–2020 era? I would say two things: the extremist discussion of racism has moved from the leftist corner of society to front and center by cloaking the argument in middle-class clothes, from the professional black man of *Get Out* who lives in an integrated area of the city to the media addressing racism as though it is a major component of every aspect of middle-class life. If you can convince white, black, Asian, and Latino middle-class voters of this tremendous ongoing white hatred in America, if you can convince whites that they are guilty of an inability to confront and control racism, you can convince them to vote socialist as there is no other way to eliminate the overarching control of white supremacism.

DAVE

I was with a group of friends getting ready to travel on a party bus to an MMA fight our buddy was participating in. The bus was parked downtown with the side door open while we waited for the last few stragglers to arrive. I was sitting up front on the partition between the rear seats and the driver and passenger seats up front. Randomly, a middle-aged white lady walking by stuck her head in the door and began to chat us up, curious as to what we were doing. She was pleasant, maybe a little kooky, but nonetheless, we entertained her questions as to what we were up to. Then, turning to me, she asked, "Are you the driver?" Looking at her sternly, I asked, "What, because I'm black?" She started gasping, her face contorted in horror, unable to find a response. Eventually she found her tongue and began to profusely profess that she was not racist and in no way was her question motivated by prejudice. She was met with howls of laughter by me and friends. Embarrassed and little annoyed, she told us to have fun and scampered off.

As amusing as this was for me and my friends, her behavior represents the attitude and sentiment of a lot of white people. At the slightest implication of racial bias or prejudice, they worry they will get the scarlet letter "R" stamped on their forehead. The paranoia that an innocuous question or statement will be misconstrued is a legitimate fear too. During the George Floyd riots, even condemning the looting on social media by whites, even very liberal whites, was met with derision and accusations of white privilege. Mass violence and destruction was excused as a legitimate expression of black rage—never mind that a substantial number of those looting and rioting were white. A country cannot survive if this level of destruction is excused and permitted. The only way I can describe it is absolute insanity.

Perhaps this can clue us in to the real intent of pushing white fragility. The intent of the Far Left is to so neuter the white majority in the United States that they voluntarily acquiesce to their political goals. No matter how good a person you are, how hard you try to be fair and equitable, it is not enough. You can humiliate yourself and your family by chaining up yourself and your kids, by participating in slave reenactments, by throwing up a BLM fist on your Facebook account, whatever you think makes you compassionate and not a bigot. But it won't be enough. The goal of those who push white fragility and other nascent far-left racial ideologies is not racial harmony; it is political revolution aimed at disrupting and destroying the current political system. That has been the stated pathway for Marxist organizations throughout the world for the last one hundred years. Their belief holds that political change can only be done through the destruction of the current bourgeois system. They require foot soldiers to throw bricks through windows and set fire to buildings. They need BLM and Antifa. What kind of opportunity will do to set things off? George Floyd's death, a black man's death, in May of 2020, during his arrest by a white policeman. Here was an opportunity that couldn't be ignored. The country had been on lockdown for two months, people were bored, frustrated, angry, and ready to explode, and here came what ostensibly seemed to be a straightforward case of police misconduct; the call for justice was immediate.

Two important issues during this frenzy were ignored and outright misrepresented. First, the prevalence of the shooting of unarmed black men. Were one to watch the media, you would think that this was an everyday occurrence with black corpses littering the streets with white police officers standing over them. The data, however, shows a different story. Unarmed black men shot by the police is in fact a rare occurrence. In 2017, seventeen unarmed black men were shot by the police. But that number doesn't tell the full story. In a few of those cases, the "victim" told the police that he had a weapon. The cops believed him. And unarmed doesn't mean harmless. One death involved an alleged attempt by the perpetrator to ram the police with his vehicle. Once again, the headline without context doesn't tell the full story. Looking deeper, we find that each shooting is unique in its circumstances. This is why it is imperative that we don't rush to judgment. Let all the facts come out, let an investigation be done. Sometimes the wheel of justice does move slowly, but it does move. [8]

Secondly, and this may be an even more important issue, is that of the judicial process. Everyone, regardless of how heinous their crime or how obvious we think their guilt may be, deserves their day in court. We are so quick as a society to cast judgement based on a short video recording taken by a bystander, yet often we only see part of the encounter. Context can be lost, and evidence that could shape the event differently may have yet to be collected and analyzed. Blacks were lynched in the old South based on allegations that were later discovered to be false. Predetermining guilt in the media and the public

---

8.   John Sullivan, Zane Anthony. "Nationwide, Police Shot and Killed Nearly 1,000 People in 2017." The Washington Post. WP Company, January 7, 2018. https://www. washingtonpost.com/investigations/nationwide-police-shot-and-killed-nearly-1000-people-in-2017/2018/01/04/4eed5f34-e4e9-11e7-ab50-621fe0588340_story.html.

arena amounts to a new type lynching where we remove from an individual the prospect of an unbiased and fair trial.

But it was an opportunity for the Left to make their move. With the help of the coronavirus lockdown, the economy tanking, and people out of work and fearful, it was the perfect storm. "You never want a serious crisis go to waste," as Rahm Emanuel once said, paraphrasing leftist Saul Alinsky, who wrote *Rules for Radicals*, and they sure as hell didn't.[9] This time, they went all out and tried to destroy the entire nation.

What betrays their intent is that white voices are not the only voices they wish to suppress. "Black people have been oppressed and silenced and their voices need to be heard" is their refrain. But when black voices spoke out against the protests and riots set off by Floyd's death, they were told they were traitors to their race and to "the cause." And what about my voice? Do I have the right as a person of color to speak out and have an opinion if it differs from the Left? Does Alan Keyes or Clarence Thomas? Have they given Thomas Sowell a platform to express his opinions? Of course not. So, let us be clear. Black voices matter and should unquestionably be heard, but let it be *all* black voices and not just the black voices of far-left Marxists.

9.   Bellune, Jerry. "Never Let a Crisis go to Waste." *Lexington County Chronicle.* Last modified March 26, 2020. https://www.lexingtonchronicle.com/business/never-let-crisis-go-waste.

CHAPTER FOUR

TRAYVON MARTIN AND BLACK LIVES MATTER

THE NEW BLACK POWER MOVEMENT AND EVERYONE OF COLOR IS A VICTIM

> "Let us be dissatisfied until that day when nobody will shout 'White Power!' – when nobody will shout 'Black Power!' – but everybody will talk about God's power and human power."
>
> MARTIN LUTHER KING, JR.[1]

President Barack Obama famously stated, "If I had a son, he would look like Trayvon." Actually, probably not exactly, as Obama's son would be one-quarter white. But, then, if Obama had married a white woman and had a son, he would look like George. What does the fact that Obama could have had a son that would be labeled a person of color have to do with Trayvon Martin getting killed? Is he saying he would also have a son who was up to no good? A son who would have been suspended from school, done drugs, would have an interest in

---

1.   Hughes, Coleman. "Martin Luther King, Colorblind Radical." *WSJ Opinion.* Last modified January 17, 2019. https://www.wsj.com/articles/martin-luther-king-colorblind-radical-11547769741.

guns, possibly have been a burglar, and would have assaulted people? Wow!

PAT

I never once thought Trayvon Martin could be my son. I would expect a son of mine to behave a lot better. I certainly would not brag about the possibility just to make a point about racism. After all, if I had married a Latino guy, George might have been my son, too. Why was President Obama making this a personal thing, making Trayvon Martin out to be a victim of a racial profiling hate crime when George Zimmerman was found not guilty of committing any crime at all? True, he might have been an overly vigilant neighborhood watch guy with a bit of a personality disorder, but it was determined he was assaulted by Trayvon and defended himself. One doesn't have to particularly like George Zimmerman or dislike Trayvon Martin to accept that the analysis of the crime was valid.

What made President Obama decide to jump in and agree with those accusing Zimmerman and whites and the police of racial discrimination and unequal treatment of blacks? Why did Obama take this stance instead of encouraging citizens to be rational when the evidence did not support a conviction of Zimmerman? Why did President Obama also not stand firm on Ferguson as another example of unfair characterization of the police and whites? It seems President Obama wanted to prove himself to the black community, to prove he was really a black man (while he was really biracial), all the while denigrating whites (as if he *wasn't* biracial)! Why didn't this mixed-race president bring the races together as one would expect? Why didn't this president encourage citizens to be objective when examining police shootings and other news stories where it is claimed that driving or walking or shopping while black led to some kind of incident? Why wasn't he the president of reason instead of race-baiting? Was he the cause or the symptom of this downward spiral into this new race war?

DAVE

The Hat

One of the downsides of being a black conservative is that there is never a shortage of "caring" white liberals who want to empathize with you due to your victim status. A pat on the back or a kind word to let you know that they are sorry for your struggle. Well-intentioned, but irritating nonetheless. One incident occurred during the riots in Baltimore, Maryland, in protest of the death of Freddy Gray in 2015, a local crack dealer who broke his neck while being transported to jail. Like other riots in recent memory, the "victim" was a criminal engaging in criminal behavior. This is not to imply that they deserved to die, but it's frustrating that so much energy is spent on memorializing those who are doing the most damage to their communities. As Baltimore burned, many wore Baltimore caps in solidarity with the protesters and in protest of the Baltimore police. I never thought much of it until I was walking through an apartment building in Washington, DC, where I was working on a solar project. One of the residents, an elderly white lady, saw my Baltimore Orioles hat and stopped me as I walked.

"I'm sorry for what's happening in Baltimore. It's very sad," she told me. For a moment, I was perplexed as to why she stopped me but then realized it was my baseball cap. Here I am, a lifelong Orioles fan wearing a ball cap to protect my balding head from sunburn (yes, given enough time, I can sunburn) and to support my local ball club, and now I'm a social justice warrior? Who else thought I was protesting? I wasn't going to find out. The next day, I started wearing my Dallas Cowboys hat. Better people think I'm an asshole than an SJW—that is, a social justice warrior.

People need to be aware of something called "unintended consequences." Sometimes when one thinks one is making things better through some kind of protest or action, there can be unfortunate outcomes that do damage to our society that may be a worse result in the long run than the original issue. One program that has been long-running in our country as an effort to protect our citizens—especially our children—is "If You See Something, Say Something." The phrase has been advertised to our citizenry as a way to help stop terrorism and protect our neighborhoods. "Neighborhood Watch" is another version of this. We used to be proud that we, as citizens, could be proactive and save our fellow man from harm. If we should see a suspicious person or object, we would call and report this to the authorities and, perhaps, thwart a terrorist attack, a kidnapping of a child or a young woman, a gang assault, a burglary, or an act of vandalism. Sure, sometimes there was that annoying busybody that was overly suspicious and jumped to conclusions, but if we want people to watch out for each other, that unintended consequence is minimal. Or at least it used to be.

The Lady with the Bullhorn

I was sitting in my car, listening to the radio and waiting for my mother to leave her friend's house. Her car was in the shop, so she needed me to give her rides for a couple of days, and, being the dutiful son, I came to pick her up. On this occasion, she was likely saying some extended goodbyes. Of course, honking the horn will only get you an earful, so better just to flip on the radio, get comfortable, and wait until she comes out. A few minutes passed by, and my mind began to wander while staring off into space. Then the piercing sound of a horn snapped me to attention. I looked out the passenger window to see an elderly lady with airhorn in one hand and her phone in the other. I knew before I rolled the window down what was happening. The neighborhood wasn't a bad neighborhood, but it was right next to some pretty sketchy areas that have a lot of gang activity. In recent months, it seemed some of the action might be moving onto this street. And here I was, a young black man just sitting in front of this lady's house in a car she didn't recognize with no obvious reason for being there. She had seen this script before. At any moment, another car would pull up. Someone would get out and get in the other car. After a few minutes, that person would return to their car, and both cars would leave. Drug Dealing 101. I fit the profile and fit the behavior, and so, I got the airhorn. This is where one has two choices: get pissed off and angrily confront the person or understand her reasoning and work it out amicably. I rolled down the window and politely said hello and stated why I was there. She explained to me, as I expected, that there was a lot of drug dealing activity in front of her house and it was extremely frustrating to her. I told her I understood her concern and suspicion, and within the course of our short conversation, she was reassured as to why I was there. By the time she bid me goodnight and went back inside, we were on friendly terms. Problem solved.

In hindsight, should I have been angry? Was she racist? For me, the answer is no and no. If anything, I'm angry at the people who look like me in that neighborhood who are engaged in criminal behavior. And as for her being racist, I could tell just by the area I was in and her mannerism and dress that she is far from being a racist. In fact, that area is very liberal, uber liberal, the granola eating kind of liberal. That's what she was, an older, uber liberal, suburban DC native who is probably a little wacky. But if I were a scumbag, my reaction could have been violent. It takes quite a bit of gumption to confront someone whom you suspect could be dangerous and capable of God knows what, so I have to give that lady some credit! My approach in situations like that one is to *profile* the situation to determine if I should be upset or offended with someone's actions. Her concern was not unreasonable in that circumstance. Now, if I were walking through the supermarket parking lot pushing a shopping cart full of groceries and she gave me the airhorn, then yes, I would be pissed. Her actions in that situation would be unreasonable.

Sometimes life is unfair and the truth inconvenient. As a black male, I am part of a group that commits violent crimes at a rate that far outpaces every other group. It's sad, and it seems that this problem will never get solved. Regardless of what the solution is, we at the very least must acknowledge its existence. And until the black crime rate falls into parity with the rest of society, I understand that it is basic human nature to preserve oneself and that I will occasionally be profiled. It doesn't offend me, and when it does happen, I deal with that person calmly and openly, and very quickly, their attitude becomes friendly and apologetic. Getting angry and confrontational might satisfy some desire to address a perceived slight, but in the long run, it accomplishes nothing and only adds to the toxicity.

PAT

I wish that same lady with the bullhorn had been home the day my friend was assaulted. The very lady I was visiting when my son was "accosted" by the woman with the bullhorn was robbed right outside her house at the exact location where my son had parked his vehicle. As she arrived home, she parked her car and was getting out, chatting on the phone with a friend, purse in hand, when a man suddenly threw an arm around her and put a knife to her throat. Her phone fell to the ground, which was incredibly fortunate because her friend on the other end of the line heard something odd going on and called my friend's sister inside the house who then called the police. Meanwhile, my friend went through a terrifying experience. (I won't go into details for privacy reasons and because it's no one's business, but it was far more traumatic than I am detailing here.) Let me just say, we don't know if the criminal was planning to sexually assault her as well but was prevented from continuing when he heard sirens approaching.

That scumbag happened to be black. So, bullhorn lady who saw something and went to say something to my son wasn't necessarily racial profiling. She simply saw an unknown man sitting in a car and didn't know if he was up to no good. He could have been the man who later attacked my friend. Because my son is a rational person who understands that people wish to keep their neighborhoods safe, he was polite to the lady and nothing bad happened. But just imagine if he had had the attitude of Trayvon Martin. A whole different scenario might have occurred. And a simple neighborhood watch moment might have turned into another Black Lives Matter outrage when it didn't need to end up that way. And my son could have ended up dead.

Now, suppose a white person sees a black man pulling a screaming white child into a car. Should they say something? Or will they be accused of racial profiling? After all, why should that white person assume a black man can't have a white child or be caring for a white child?

Do you know how often people asked me if I was babysitting when I was at the park with my nonwhite children? Latinas often get asked that question when they actually *are* taking care of the children of white families, so why shouldn't I get that question in return? Sometimes it is just natural for people to ask that kind of question because they are curious or just trying to get straight in their mind what the situation is. White parents of adopted Chinese kids get this a lot, too. One time, my black son was at church summer camp and the ladies who ran the program were very cautious about releasing the children at the end of the day. They would not open the door to let a child out unless they were sure that the person arriving was a parent. My son Jeremy looked through the window in the door and saw me coming up the walk.

He told the lady, "There's my Mom!"

The lady looked out. "No, it's not."

He said, "Yes, it is!"

The lady said, "No, it's not."

I knocked on the door. The lady opened it and asked what I wanted as there was only one kid left, the black one.

"Yes?" The lady looked at me.

I pointed to Jeremy. "My son."

Jeremy grinned at the lady. "I told you!"

The lady looked abashed. "Sorry!"

That night at the dinner table, we went back and forth.

"That's my Mom!"

"No, it's not!"

"Yes, it is!"

"No, it's not!"

We laughed. We thought it was pretty funny.

In reality, that woman was doing her job and protecting the children. There was no reason for me to get mad at her.

Now, suppose a PONEC (Person of Not Enough Color) little girl is shrieking and her black grandfather is stuffing her into a vehicle and some person calls the police. Should her grandfather get all bent out of shape? What if someone saw that happening and it wasn't her grandfather who was shoving her screaming into a vehicle? Would we all be horrified that no one did anything? Sure, we would, and we would be shouting to the hills that no one cared enough to save her. Sometimes, if something seems off, people will call the police on a white man with a white child or a black man with a black child. We don't hear about these cases because we cannot assign racism to them. But, oh my God, let it be a concerned white citizen calling on a black person, and it's got to be a racist thing!

Yes, there are people who are racist who might do such a thing. And there are also white assholes who complain to the police when they see black people doing something that they didn't like (like the woman who called the police about a black family picnicking in a questionable location or the white lady who got all mad because a mixed-race couple was taking photos of their kid in the middle of a path in an area she deemed was not for the public to use or block; these two videos went viral on YouTube). But sometimes, that white person has called the police on white people as well, yet, we don't hear about that. We also don't hear when black people call the police on white people! You don't think there are black people who think some shady white person may be up to no good?

So we have YouTube videos and tweets and Facebook pages and news stories about how white people are accusing black people of things all over the country because of our horrible, racist society when, in fact, most of the stories aren't really racist at all, and the few that are, well, so there are a few racist idiots somewhere in this wide country of ours. Go figure. People aren't perfect. The problem is, incidents like these used to happen in a community, and it was just a community issue. Now, each incident—the one in a small town in Kentucky or upstate New York or in Texas or Florida—becomes a national story and is said to represent not one fool in one isolated place, but an entire race.

So, "If You See Something, Say Something," is it worth it? Is it worth being accused of hating blacks or hating Muslims, being doxed, and having one's life and one's family's life ruined if the incident one reports turns out to be nothing? Many people have become reluctant to report anything or do anything for fear of becoming a pariah or even ending up in court like George Zimmerman, or worse, prison. So, the unintended consequences of being overly sensitive about race and racial profiling is less vigilance and less reporting of possible terrorists, serial predators, and burglars. We as citizens can no longer speak up because speaking up is far too risky.

DAVE

"Yeah, some cops are assholes." Don't get mad at me; I have many friends in law enforcement who make similar proclamations, but I understand their intent. What they mean is that law enforcement is a very stressful job where they put their lives at risk every day dealing with the least reputable people in our society. To make it through the day, much less a twenty-year career, you must have an edge, some callousness, some "attitude;" otherwise, you would simply go crazy. It's no wonder that law enforcement officers suffer high rates of divorce and alcoholism. Simply put, being a cop is a tough gig. This is something I understand, and perhaps that is why I've never had issues with the police. Oh, I've been pulled over plenty of times, but never for "being black"—not to say that it has never happened to some people of color. It has.

However, in my case, I can't say that there wasn't a legitimate reason for being pulled over. Most of the time, I was let off with a warning; only a few times was I ticketed. Looking back, it could have been much worse had I not followed two basic rules: be polite and follow instructions. I didn't catch an attitude, talk back, get defensive, or immediately jump to the conclusion that I was being targeted for the color of my skin. Instead, I bore them to death. You can always see a level of apprehension when a cop pulls you over, especially at night, but after a short interaction, you can visibly see their body language change—from suspicious and grumpy to just plain grumpy. "Yes, sir," "no, sir," "thank you, sir," "goodnight, sir." Only when the window is up and I'm a mile down the road do I drop profanities and bitch about how much beer money I'm about to send to the state. This is a basic concept that I find far too many of my fellow people of color fail to understand. If you look for racism, you're going to find it, real or imagined. Don't confused a racist asshole with someone who is just an asshole.

PAT

It's not like only people of color have uncomfortable experiences with police officers pulling them over. I am a sixty-five-year-old woman driving a red Mazda Miata convertible—hardly a drug dealer car—and I have been pulled over a number of times and had to deal with law enforcement.

I remember one night I got pulled over by two cops. The first one was a white cop who must have graduated the academy the day before. He never cracked a smile (okay, maybe my jokes didn't deserve it) and was a by-the-book guy who looked like he had a stick up his ass. But, regardless, I had turned on my light inside the car, both of my hands were on the steering wheel, and I asked permission before I reached for anything. Years ago, I had taken a class by Massad Ayoob, one of the leading police firearms trainers in the country, and I experienced those tests of "Shoot, Don't Shoot," where films are shown and one has just a second to decide if the person is pulling a weapon on you. I failed a bunch of times. I shot a person reaching for a wallet and got shot by a person I thought was reaching for paperwork. This is what a cop has to deal with every time he or she pulls a person over on the side of a highway. Even an older white lady might be dangerous; so it's understandable that the police officer is extremely paranoid. Anyone who says that such caution is evidence of a cop without balls has never been in the position of trying to determine if the driver is about to kill you.

So, I moved very, very slowly with the white cop, and he gave me a warning and sent me on my way. Still never smiled, but the incident ended with no one getting hurt. Five minutes down the road, I got pulled over again for the same issue (headlight was out). This time a smiley black cop shined his light in my right window and told me he needed to do so for safety. I smiled back and told him his police mate down the road had just given me a warning. I asked permission to reach for the paper, he gave it, and I held it up. He laughed and sent me on my way. Again, bad incident averted by good behavior.

I have done a number of ride-alongs with law enforcement in one of the most dangerous areas of my county. I always went on a Friday or Saturday night so I wouldn't be bored to death. What I noted was this: the police officers went out of their way to be polite and even called criminals "sir" and "ma'am." I found their restraint commendable. I also noticed that there were two kinds of criminals: those that understood the cops were doing their job and those that were pissed off that they were. The former tended to just give up, put their hands behind their backs, get cuffed, and were taken off to jail without any problems. Often, the criminal and the cop chatted in a friendly manner, sometimes using each other's names because they had been through this drill before.

The latter caused trouble. They cussed, fought, kicked, bit, spit, and did everything they could to resist arrest. They complained they couldn't breathe while being taken down and then complained that the handcuffs were too tight. They fought every inch of the way, putting the police officers in danger. That there are not more criminals damaged in arrest and transport is surprising, and I have to credit the police officers for their restraint.

With all the complaints and charges against police officers, there are unintended consequences that are damaging the black community, making life worse for law-abiding citizens.

When law enforcement officers come under unfair condemnation and incarceration, the desire for people to join the police force declines. Who would want to take the chance of not only getting killed by a criminal but being imprisoned unfairly for a lifetime, losing one's freedom, and not being able to raise one's children? Who wants to go out on the streets to be treated like crap by the local citizenry who one is trying to protect? Not many, it appears, and therefore, there are less applicants these days applying for the police force, which is a big problem. Either there aren't enough cops on the street, or the agency has to hire less qualified people, maybe less psychologically stable people, to put a uniform on and a gun in their hands.

Is this what a struggling community needs?

I am not sure what it is about Hollywood that likes to be so divisive about race and about the police, but they have been playing this tune for years. A great example of their attempts to upset the racial apple cart and paint the police as racist brutes and the system as systemically incarcerating innocent black men is the movie *The Hurricane*, the story of boxer Rubin Carter, played by Denzel Washington, which came out in 1999. Of course, I went to see it with great enthusiasm, with a positive attitude, having read many good reviews praising the film. After the fact, I was so appalled, so stunned as a criminal profiler (this movie was way ahead of the Netflix *Making a Murderer* travesty, but the push behind it wasn't so much for money and ratings as for making a political statement...facts be damned... not surprising coming out of Hollywood) that I wrote this blog post profiling the crime and the movie.

THE HURRICANE - ODE TO A PSYCHOPATH

I had heard the name Rubin "Hurricane" Carter some-time back in the 1970s, but couldn't quite remember why. So, when the movie, The Hurricane *came out, I rushed out to see it. It was definitely a movie that I HAD to see because it contained to a number of elements I was very well acquainted with and very concerned about: injustice, racism, and boxing. I have raised two mixed race children and one adopted black son over the last twenty years and my husband has struggled with some forms of racism in his work and in the community, dealing with this American dilemma ever since his arrival here from Jamaica in his teens. Boxing? Oh, yeah...I know boxing. I watched the rise and fall of my brother-in-law and three-time world champion, Simon Brown. I spent quite a few evenings ringside in Atlantic City and more than a few evenings cussing out Don King and a host of other ethically chal-lenged promoters. Yes, I was more than excited this movie came out. I was looking forward to hearing the story and struggle for justice by this boxer whose name I had heard, but never knew the real story of.*

My excitement lasted only a fraction of the way into this movie. For you who have not yet seen the movie, let me set up the basic events. A trio of extraordinarily caring and docile Canadians offer a home to an impoverished black American teenager and proceed to homeschool him. This happens during the 1970s and the Canadians come off like innocent do-gooders beyond belief. You can't really blame the movie (well, yes you can) because it is based, without the slightest departure, on the book written by the Canadians themselves. I guess the producers were not too concerned about a one-sided viewpoint. Anyway, the Canadians are busy homeschooling Lesra and allowing the youth to pick out his choice of reading materials when he "happens across" the book written by Rubin Carter called The Sixteenth Round. From here Lesra fascinates the whole group with his out loud readings of Carter's story of injustice and imprisonment and we are taken along with him through this historical journey.

The story begins in the movie showing Carter when he was just a tyke - he looks about eight or nine - when a serious altercation occurs that gets him sent to reform school for the rest of his youth. He and his friends are playing by a waterfall when a middle-aged white child molester attempts to lure one of the little boys with his gold watch. When he attempts to grab the little boy, Carter, trying to save his friend, throws a bottle and hits the man on the head. The man then turns to Carter and grabs him and tries to toss him off a cliff. Carter pulls out his Scout knife, stabs the man and the man drops him. Then Carter is pulled into the police station and an evil, racist, really nasty policeman, scares and abuses the little boy and then the little boy is sent away for his act of self-defense. I think I actually started laughing out loud much to the horror of my neighboring moviegoers. I watched the rest of the movie about the "railroading of Rubin Carter" snickering into my popcorn and rolling my eyes. I left the theatre shaking my head while everyone else shouted and clapped at Carter's victory and release from prison.

What was wrong with this picture? How could the supporters of Rubin Carter convince me he was guilty while trying to convince me he wasn't? When I talked to others and read the web sites, I found only one person who felt as I did. I began to wonder if I had misinterpreted some-thing from the film. So I went out and bought the books, Lazarus *and* The Hurricane *written by Sam Chaiton and Terry Swinton (of the Canadian group), and Rubin Carter's own book* The Sixteenth Round. *The Canadians' book offered nothing new, as it was almost word for word the movie. However, it at least gave me a nice working script of the picture. I also watched the movie again to see why I thought it was a lie. The events in the movie seemed phony and lacking in details, so I moved on to Carter's own words to fill in the missing information. And there, it was…the truth, nestled within a huge pack of lies. Carter was clearly a psychopath and a pathological liar. In his own words, he tells us this. Truth and lies intermingle in a most fascinating journey through his psychopathic mind. What a gem of a book!*[2]

I will leave the extensive profiling part of the blog out, but interested readers can find it online at *The Daily Profiler.* Nevertheless, I can assure you that Hurricane Carter led a life of psychopathic violence and crime from the time he was small until the time he got convicted of first-degree murder in a triple homicide. Oddly, in his own book, he doesn't paint the police as ever treating him that badly! Don't believe everything in Wikipedia's version; their information comes from the book written by that little band of Communists in Canada.[3]

But, I digress. Back to my blog.

---

2.   Brown, Pat. "The Hurricane – Ode to a Psychopath." The Pat Brown Criminal Profiling Agency. Accessed July 18, 2020. http://www.patbrownprofiling.com/article1.html.

3.   "Rubin Carter." Wikipedia. Last modified July 23, 2020. https://en.wikipedia.org/wiki/Rubin_Carter.

The crime the left tries to exonerate him of was a robbery of the Lafayette Grill where people were shot dead when the bartender threw a bottle at the two armed men as they entered (a crime Carter most likely was the mastermind of and was probably the getaway driver).

So, Carter gets convicted and continues his violence in prison. He writes this fascinating book, which is chosen by the Canadians as a good protest and publicity campaign against the U.S. government. Lots of celebrities jump on board because no one really cares to search for the truth. Carter served a purpose for their platforms and they in turn were useful for Carter. For psychopaths, "people are either useful or in the way." For Carter, the Canadians were most useful until he got out. Eventually, they got in his way, and he moved on. Now, with the advent of this movie, all come together for another joyful purpose! Making money! Except for Artis, who after a stint as a youth counselor in Virginia, got sent back to prison for some…er…drug thing.

All I can say is, thank God this movie didn't get any awards. Denzel wasn't bad, but the movie was childish, and, of course, a total fabrication of Carter's mind and the Canadians and a travesty against history and the victims of his crime. There are innocent people in jail who were railroaded for crimes they didn't commit, but, for God's sake, why does Hollywood find it necessary to ignore them and instead glorify vicious criminals? For a truly sad account of a black man who was railroaded by politics and police corruption, read The Doctor, the Murder, the Mystery: The true Story of the Dr. John Banion Murder Case *by Barbara D'Amato.*

Hurricane's "story" can't hold a candle to this man and the injustice committed against him. Too bad Hollywood didn't try a little harder to find real history and a real hero.[4]

---

4.   Brown, Pat. "The Hurricane – Ode to a Psychopath." The Pat Brown Criminal Profiling Agency. Accessed July 18, 2020. http://www.patbrownprofiling.com/article1.html.

It seems that the Left finds it necessary to keep the racial war going. If they don't have a real martyr, they will create one. Just when things are rather peaceful, here they go again revving up the anger and hate. We need to remember our history—even the bad stuff—for just as the Jews remind us all to "never forget" about the Holocaust, we should never forget about the enslavement of a whole group of people simply because of their color or weakness in the political structure; however, remembering is not the same as finding or fabricating cases of racism in order to fuel discontent and disrupt progress. We should always speak up against anyone who does this. Unfortunately, it is a difficult thing to do. When I wrote this blog about Rubin Carter, even though I pointed out that I was sympathetic to the fight against racism, that I knew the boxing world, and that I was married to a black man (at the time), the vicious emails and comments I got calling me a racist because I refused to believe in Carter's innocence was astounding. Certainly, very little has been written in the general media, few have spoken up, because they don't dare do so for fear of being called a racist or an Uncle Tom. That was 1999, and twenty years later, people are still afraid to speak up.

DAVE

We hear constantly from pundits across the progressive media that we need honest conversation about race, yet it is perhaps the most disingenuous call for national dialogue of any topic. Of course, what they really want is capitulation to their viewpoint and any disagreement with it is automatically labeled racist. In a weird role reversal, it is black conservatives who are put in the awkward position of having to coax whites into participating in this conversation with assurances that they won't be accused of racism. And our own position doesn't come with impunity. You will get called an Uncle Tom by some other blacks and, surprisingly, even accused of being racist yourself by some of the more self-righteous white progressives. It's really quite astonishing and a bit surreal when it happens (and it does). Perhaps the most common criticism I've heard is that you as a black person, for some inexplicable reason, don't realize that you're oppressed. It reminds me of the scene from *Monty Python and the Holy Grail* where a cart full of dead bodies is being pulled through a plague-ridden town with the call to the townspeople to "bring out your dead!" One townsman walks up with an old man slung over his shoulders who is very much alive, but nevertheless the townsman wants to toss him in the cart. "I'm not dead!" the old man protests. "He says he's not dead," the morgue worker repeats to the townsman. "Yes, he is," says the townsman. This dispute continues until its comical resolution when the old man is struck over the head by the townsman so there is no question of him being dead and is *then* tossed into the cart. Like the man who believed he was alive when others denied that perception, if you are black, you are a victim whether you think you are one or not.

Black victimhood is a necessary prerequisite for the continuity of progressive thought. How can you be a social justice warrior if there is no war to fight? Strangely, for a group that makes fighting for racial justice their ultimate goal, the existence of equality would render their movement obsolete. This explains why progressives can be particularly spiteful toward black conservatives. If black conservatives succeed in convincing enough blacks to drop the cloak of victimhood, the progressive model collapses like a house of cards. Progressivism needs victims and oppressors, and if you don't have victims, you don't have oppressors. White guilt begins to fade away, people start to get along, and we become a stronger, more cohesive society.

Why are victims, oppressors, and heightened racial awareness such a large part of progressivism? The answer is pretty obvious if one ignores the gnashing of progressive teeth when bringing up Marxism. Whether you read Marx, Lenin, or Trotsky, their overarching theme is inequality among groups. In classical Marxism, it's the evil owners of the means of production that exploit the worker. There is always an oppressor, and there is always a victim. If you worked in a factory in Europe in the late nineteenth century, no doubt at some point you were handed a pamphlet by a Marxist rabble-rouser, encouraging you to join the movement and fight against those who exploit you for your labor. In most European countries, this never gained enough traction to overthrow the governments. Unfortunately for Russia, Trotsky and Lenin were successful, with the latter giving birth to the age of Stalin. When one looks back and analyzes why Marx was unsuccessful in sparking revolution in the large European powers, it was in part due to the fact that while working conditions were tough, at least men were able to provide for their families. If people are not convinced that they have nothing to lose, they are not as malleable to committing to drastic change and uprooting society. The more stability a country has, the harder it is to convince the citizens to rock the boat. Likewise, in modern times, economic prosperity thwarts the progressive ideology. Chaos, confusion, and division are stoked. Racial incidences magnified and splashed for days on the front pages of the newspapers. In order to kick-start the next leftward lurch, we need to be divided.

How can one not notice this game being played in the media? If a white guy is shot by the cops, the headline will be,

"Cops shoot man." If the victim is black and the officer white, the headline reads, "Black man killed by white police officer." You have to get to the third paragraph to find out the "victim" was a repeat offender who is caught on the officer's body cam pointing a weapon at the cop. This doesn't just happen on rare occasions. If you were to dig through newspapers over the last several years, you would see this trend repeat itself over and over and over again. Does this sound like behavior of people who want an honest discussion about race? And what is more frustrating is that there *are* legitimate cases of people of color shot by the police in questionable circumstances, yet these seem to get ignored. Throw in a lie like "hands up, don't shoot," and you have a nice catchphrase for Black Lives Matter to chant. These blatant acts of propaganda by the media are not only damaging to the police but paint black people as a group supportive of violent criminals. And there are two sides to this coin. White people are once again guilty through their racial connection to the "racist" and "predatory" cop who was looking for an excuse to kill a person of color.

PAT

I don't want my kids to think of themselves as victims. Too often that kind of thinking assumes there is only one answer to a problem instead of a multitude. I remember telling my boys that there was a reason some old lady in the neighborhood might be scared of them when they were teenagers walking down the street, and it had nothing to do with being black or biracial. I can't tell you how many times I have heard that story about how white people were scared of black people if they got into an elevator together or were walking down a quiet street together. The assumption was, "It happened because I am black. I am a victim." But, maybe, there was another reason, and if one can get out of the victim mentality for a minute, one can examine if there is another reason.

Picture this: You are a white person walking down a street. You come to the end and only have two choices: left or right. To the left is a group of six black men, and to the right is a group of six white men. Which way do you go? Now, without further information, the white person might say, "To the right." Then, blacks might say, "See? Racist!" But, now suppose I tell you that the six black men to the left were Jehovah's Witnesses dressed in suits and the six white men to the right were tatted up and dressed in thug clothes and bandannas. I bet most white people would choose to go toward the six black men. So, in this case, race would not have been a factor.

So, I told my two boys, if you are walking down the street looking like thugs, walking like you are questionable characters, with a mean look on your faces, sure, that old white lady might get freaked (and so might that old black lady). But, if you are dressed nicely, walking normally, and smiling, my guess is the old white lady will simply nod and wish you "good morning."

Sometimes one makes themselves a victim in one's own eyes. When society makes out people of a certain race to be victims all the time or oppressors all the time, no one wins.

CHAPTER FIVE

MEDIA MIND CONTROL

HOLLYWOOD, TELEVISION PROGRAMMING,
AND THE CABLE NEWS NETWORKS

"No lie can live forever."

MARTIN LUTHER KING, JR.[1]

There is no question that propaganda has been with us since the beginning of time. No doubt the first men who returned from hunting empty-handed came up with a good story as to why they failed so that the rest of the cavemen and cavewomen didn't withhold from them the roots and nuts they had been gathering all day. As the population increased and civilizations grew into villages and cities and countries, those in power found numerous ways to control their subjects, either through physical or psychological means.

History is written by the victors and rewritten by those who have the ability and access to manipulate the minds of the citizens. What is "true" is often regulated by those who disseminate

---

1.   Raab, Nathan. "10 People Who Inspired Martin Luther King (And He Hoped Would Inspire Us)." *Forbes*. Last modified January 20, 2014. https://www.forbes.com/sites/nathanraab/2014/01/20/10-people-who-inspired-martin-luther-king-and-he-hoped-would-inspire-us/#48c8969379c2.

"facts" and by how gullible the people receiving the information are. The question of quantity is also a large factor as to how the masses accept the information as factual as opposed to fake. Like gossip, if only one person tells the story, that story is probably questioned by those receiving the information, especially if the gossiper is not the most credible character. But the more people who tell the story and the more persuasive they are, the more the story becomes probable. If a very esteemed person repeats the story, it may become gospel and unacceptable to question its validity. If a person less acceptable to the public speaks in opposition, character assassination can elevate the original story to a level of acceptance by way of not wanting guilt by association with the naysayer. A master of propaganda knows how to exploit all the avenues of information dissemination to achieve the highest level of success in controlling information to the public.

PAT

A great example of control of information through the ages, and how it changes with who controls the avenue of information, is the history of Cleopatra. At the time, when the last queen of Egypt died on August 12, 30 BC, and word of her demise went out to the citizens of Alexandria and then back to Rome. The one controlling the details of the pharaoh's death was the man who had held her captive, Octavian, the last Roman conqueror standing and the new dictator for life of the Roman Empire. Cleopatra's husband, Antony, had died before Cleopatra, and when Cleopatra died, the only witnesses—her handmaidens—died with her. So, the story of exactly *how* the queen died lay solely in the voice of Octavian. He claimed she committed suicide by an asp, a manner of death that would seem an honorable and brave ending, as well as a religiously symbolic one, for the highly beloved last ruler of Egypt. What Octavian actually told the masses at the time is not known as we do not have his words, but his behavior during the days after his invasion of Egypt with his armies and navy—ingratiating himself just prior to her demise by spending much time chatting with the elites of Alexandria—would lead one to conclude that dragging Cleopatra through the streets of Rome in a triumph or brutally murdering her might not go over well with the people Octavian was trying to impress in order to have a smooth transition of government into his hands.

And, so the story began that Cleopatra and her hand-maidens smuggled a cobra into the tomb where they were imprisoned and killed themselves with the reptile. And the transition of government appeared to have gone as Octavian wished. Then, the story was carried on by way of Plutarch, who added romantic and fantastical details to the account of Cleopatra's last days, as he socialized with the highest echelons of the Roman elite and, therefore, Greek though he was born, it behooved him to elevate the characters of the Roman leaders and denigrate their enemies. In this case, Cleopatra and Antony. So, Cleopatra became a vamp, Antony a love-struck fool, and Octavian, well, not such a bad guy.

Interestingly, this story by Plutarch—who I call the Dan Brown of his time, an author who knew how to captivate his audience with a great story—stuck for the next 2000 years. He is called an ancient historian and revered by academics who seem to relish in the retelling of such colorful stories as they 1) sell books, and 2) don't disturb the academic world by questioning all the historians who came before.

I ended up being the first person in centuries to refute Plutarch's version of Cleopatra's life and death, and I achieved something of a miracle in ridding the Cleopatra story of the snake. How did I do this? Did I write my theory on a blog read by a few thousand and was so convincing that readers spread the word of my theory and it made its way throughout the academic world, winning everyone over? Did I write a book and the historians and Egyptologists saw the logic and changed their minds, then wrote of this new analysis by the criminal profiler Pat Brown? No, none of that happened.

What happened was TV. Television. The new, very effective disseminator of "truth" and, to many viewers, a very visible, convincing medium. Books can still be effective if they are distributed by a major publisher, get great publicity, and receive many top reviews. But television has the odd charm of being able to implant pictures in people's heads, add music to stir emotions, and, quite frankly, promote a one-sided agenda in a most clever manner. It is a powerful tool, and those in television know this. If one adds the phrase "Discovery Channel" before the program title (in this case, *The Mysterious Death of Cleopatra*), it becomes a trusted disseminator of history.

And so, I presented my theory on this show, walking about Egypt flanked by well-known historians and Egyptologists, and had my analysis brought to life with 3D depictions and reenactments, and it made sense to the viewers. Plutarch was finally trumped. Even historians watching the show accepted my conclusion that the snake as the dispatcher of Cleopatra was not very credible. They went on to write books with the snake removed (no mention of Pat Brown doing the removing), and now Plutarch's version is long gone. I went on to write a book, *The Murder of Cleopatra*, demolishing the rest of Plutarch's creative fiction about the queen's life and death. Yet because it was published by a small company and has not been given the television treatment, this well-researched and documented analysis has yet to get much support. In fact, because I am not part of academia, the character assassination showed up quite quickly to put down my work. But I bet if a four-to-six part series by the Discovery Channel or the History Channel comes out with my theories about Cleopatra's full story as ruler of Egypt, we would see things change in short order because television has a power to reach the masses in a way unprecedented in history.

Netflix is solid proof of this. *Making a Murderer* is by far the most successful true crime series ever put out, and it has been very profitable for the company. That it is a completely manipulative piece of garbage that frames a murderer (pun intended) as an innocent is a frightening look at how dangerous propaganda can be. In spite of the prosecution presenting an airtight case with a mountain of evidence and a jury convicting Steven Avery in the brutal sexual murder of a young woman, Netflix managed to present their show completely from the defense's point of view. And, in doing so, they have managed to convince an incredibly huge number of viewers that Steven Avery—a man who once doused his cat in oil and threw it into a fire for the fun of it, a man who called the victim to his house on a ruse just before she went missing, a man whose fire pit contained the victim's bones, on whose lot the victim's car was found, and in whose house the victim's car key was found, a man whose own nephew confessed to helping his uncle dispatch the woman— is innocent. That is, in spite of all of the above, many citizens of the United States are clamoring for Steven Avery, a sexual psychopathic killer, to be freed—all because the television show convinced them of his innocence.

That is the power of television.

And it is the power of television news as well. Many people think that the news is somehow objective, that facts are given, and that experts are brought on to give their particular viewpoint in a fair-minded fashion. Nothing could be further from the truth. There is something called a pre-interview that most experts get before finalizing their appearance on the show. In that interview, the expert is asked what he thinks. If he thinks something different than what the news show wishes to promote, suddenly that time slot vanishes and he is thanked and told he will be asked on another time. Or, if he *is* allowed on with a very different opinion than what is being dished out on the show, he is only being brought in as a punching bag to be mocked and torn apart by the other experts on the panel.

Viewers aren't given the facts and then allowed to make their minds up; their minds are being made up by the media, and oftentimes, they haven't a clue that they are being led down a path that has been carefully laid out for them.

DAVE

"You obviously watch Faux News." If you lean to the right, you've heard this annoying line from liberal friends or family members a dozen times. What's missed by them is the irony of their statement. When they say, "You obviously watch Faux News" and not CNN, MSNBC, CBS, ABC, or any other media outlet, they are effectively admitting that all the other media outlets lean left. While they may think they are attacking a source of right-wing propaganda, they are, in effect, admitting to the stranglehold that progressivism has on most of the major media. And you will notice that progressive fascists aren't content with controlling almost everything; they want to control everything. Notice the term "progressive fascists"—stop calling them liberals. Liberals of the past supported freedom of speech, due process, and tolerance of all viewpoints. The modern "liberal" does not.

But to understand why the media is so completely biased we must look at the bigger picture. Who owns these news platforms? Massive conglomerates. CNN is owned by Time Warner, and Time Warner is owned by AT&T, a media conglomerate that has assets totaling over half a trillion dollars![2] But wait, I was told the massive corporations would favor Republicans and Republican policies. The keyword, however, is Republican policies, not conservative policies. This is why you are possibly frustrated with the Republican Party and may have voted for Trump. You've come to realize that the establishment Republican Party isn't much different from the Democratic Party. Democrats want to use government to control your life, and Republicans want to use government to protect their monopolies. Progressivism is not a threat to these corporations; in fact, they support progressivism. Do not be deceived.

PAT

Dave, you really hit on what has happened to television in general. A film that has become quite famous, *Network*, came out in 1976 and is a fantastical tale (or so we thought at the time) of television networks running amok, caring less about the truth than ratings. If you've never seen the film, which won a bunch of Oscars, it's both a fantastic satire and a messianic look at the future. In fact, it turns out to be less

---

2.   Dybek, Martin. "AT&T Inc. (NYSE:T) Balance Sheet: Assets." Stock Analysis on the Net. Last modified February 21, 2020. https://www.stock-analysis-on.net/NYSE/Company/ATT-Inc/Financial-Statement/Assets.

science fiction and black humor than a depiction of television in the last ten years.

A newsman, Howard Beale, has become severely depressed with his job, life, and the world he lives in and threatens to kill himself on air. He is to be fired and never return to air, but he convinces his producers to let him have one more night to say goodbye (without the suicide). He tells the viewers he is fed up with all the bullshit. He goes on a rant, and the ratings soar. They put him back on air as a "mad prophet," and when he tells everyone to open their windows, stick their heads out, and shout, "I am mad as hell and I'm not going to take it anymore!" the whole city goes nuts and people are screaming out windows everywhere.

Seeing the monetary advantage in crazy stuff like this, the producer starts a reality show—the first of its kind on TV (can you imagine this was something unheard of in 1976?)—and the show follows a bunch of Patty Hearst/Symbionese-style terrorists and history is made. The loss of ethics is so severe, the producer—a fabulous, cold-blooded Faye Dunaway—arranges to have the Mad Prophet assassinated on air to get rid of him when his ratings start declining and to have the top moment of the year in news.

To truly see how Paddy Chayefsky wrote a screenplay that terrifyingly imagined where television was going to be in the future and how it would affect the citizenry, let me offer some of the most eye-opening lines of the movie.[3]

"I am putting the news show under programming." (And this is exactly what has happened. Rather than a news show simply stating the news, news shows have

---

3.   Chayefsky, Paddy. *Network*. Beverly Hills, CA: Metro-Goldwyn-Mayer Studios. Film, 1976.

become programs that include question-and-answer sessions between the host and guest commentator. The program is planned to be inflammatory, eyebrow-raising, exciting, and rabble-rousing—pretty much a professional wrestling show with the winner already picked out.)

"It's about making money." (Absolutely. Journalism as a profession with a duty to inform the public for the greater good has turned into something else with twenty-four-seven news networks.)

"By October, we had 40 million shares more than any other network...." (Ratings, and the money they bring in, are what is important.)

"You people and 60,000 million people are listening to me now...because you don't read." (Ouch! How true is this today?)

"This tube can make or break Presidents." (What has the media done for President Obama and to President Trump?)

"Woe is us if it falls into the hands of the wrong people...." (Like the Democratic Party.)

"Woe is us because this company is now in the hands of CCA....and when the 12th largest company in the world controls the most awesome goddamn propaganda force in the whole godless world who knows what will be peddled for truth." (We can change the letters CCA into any other network with three letters.)

"Television is not the truth, it's entertainment, it's a circus." (I don't think this needs additional commentary.)

"We're in the boredom killing business." (And, yet, people are becoming more bored every day because they rely on entertainment to fill their time instead of hobbies and education and family.)

"You're not going to get any truth from us…we lie like hell…." (Yes, because you are fake news.)

"Banks and insurance companies are buying networks for somebody else but they won't tell you that they are buying it for Saudi Arabia. For the Arabs." (Who controls our networks now?)

"There are no nations. There are no peoples. There are no Russians. There are no Arabs. There are no third worlds. There is no West…. There is just…a multinational dominion of dollars…. The international system of currency that determines the totality of life in this planet. There is no America, there is no democracy, there is only IBM, and AT&T, DuPont, Union Carbide, and Exxon. Those are the nations of today. We no longer live in a world of nations and ideology…it is a college of corporations…. The world is a business. Our children will live to see that perfect world…all men will work for a common profit…it is a corporate cosmology and Democracy is a dying concept…the individual is finished…the whole world is becoming mass produced and programmed."

That last rant was spoken by the network director to the one newsman who actually still cared about presenting the news as news. It was quite a frightening vision this director had of a global control of money and people and of a media that would do its bidding to keep the citizenry entranced with a fake reality and by fake news. He foresaw how the media could profoundly influence the vote for representatives in our Congress and for our presidential leader with the marriage of politics and media. *Network* was a modern-day version of 1984 that no one at the time really took seriously. I hope it is not too late.

DAVE

The power of a headline is incredible. Despite being fooled so many times, I still instinctually believe that it must be truthful. There is no way a publication with the history and "prestige" of *The New York Times* or *The Washington Post* would lie, would they? Of course, as many conservatives come to opine, they lie like dogs. But even knowing that, I will scroll through the headlines of *Yahoo! News* and see what appears to be a damning headline of President Trump and click on it before I realize it is the *NYT* or the *WP*. As much as I love him, admittedly, he is capable of occasional goofy statements that make you roll your eyes and rub your forehead. That being said, almost every time I actually stop to read the content of the article, I can find the exact moment where they twisted his words or feigned stupidity in interpreting a statement. It's so brazen and in your face. Stop to think of where we would be without the internet. We now have the luxury of collectively fact-checking the media and the smears, but just a few decades ago, what the evening news said was the "truth." Newsmen like Walter Cronkite had immense power to sway public opinion. For example, his criticism of the Vietnam War was credited with helping to shift public opinion against the war effort. The news was trusted, somber, and held in high esteem. Fast-forward to the present day, and watching a CNN panel squawking over one another is barely a step up from *Jerry Springer*.

People often describe the internet as being the worst and greatest invention of mankind. That description is certainly fitting; however, the importance of the internet cannot be understated. Even as it was being developed and first introduced to the public, we didn't fully understand the power it would have as a check and balance to those who have power. Internet sleuths sitting in their basements in their underwear have exposed politicians, uncovered damning information, and collectively served as a counterbalance to mainstream propaganda. This has not gone unnoticed by the tech companies who work hand in glove with the political establishment. Working together, companies like Twitter, Facebook, and YouTube have purged their platforms of content *they* have deemed to be false information or fake news. Never mind three years of Russian collusion pushed by the mainstream media. Is there a ban coming on that? Of course not. The challenge for freedom-loving people moving forward will be to protect free speech on the internet. We must support content providers who challenge the mainstream media and help them grow their influence. With the internet, the genie is out of the bottle, and the Establishment is trying to stuff it back in. Don't let this happen. Our liberty is at stake.

Unfortunately, these platforms don't just target the "little fish." Just when we thought that the 2016 presidential campaign had the most egregious bias we've ever seen, it didn't take long for 2020 to get even worse. One of the provisions that companies like Facebook and Twitter enjoy is that they cannot be sued for hosting defamatory content; they can let news sources and private citizens post whatever they want (in theory). Since it's *your* slanderous tweet or Facebook post or the news organization's tweet or Facebook post and not theirs (as *they* are not the publisher of that material; you are when you hit the send button), you can get sued, not them. You or the mainstream media just happened to pick their service to launch whatever attack. A newspaper, on the other hand (and the television news media as well), is supposed to be legally responsible for whatever it puts out. If *The New York Times* prints a false news story that damages an individual's reputation, they can be sued. Of course, in practice, this is very difficult as the judicial system is hesitant to award damages in defamation lawsuits in part due to biases of the presiding judge, especially when the defamed person is a public figure. Even a straightforward case of character assassination and slander can be difficult to pursue. We have seen, however, one positive outcome to a lawsuit in recent times. When CNN mischaracterized the interaction between Nick Sandman of Covington Catholic High School and Native American Nathan Phillips, a lawsuit was filed against CNN by lawyers representing the student. The lawsuit was settled with CNN paying an undisclosed amount. A rare outcome for a lawsuit filed against a media company.[4]

But what is interesting about platforms is that while they can permit anything to be published (especially everything *they* like), they essentially can also censor. A bookstore can determine which books it will put on its shelves, a platform can decide which content they want to display. And this is what they have done when they are deciding what information is "correct" or "incorrect." For example, there has been a huge shutdown of any content on platforms that is anti-vaccine or that provides the viewpoint that vaccines may cause autism. The content providers have decided that "science has proven" vaccines are good and don't cause autism and, therefore, anyone putting

---

4.   Richardson, Valerie. "CNN settles $275M lawsuit with Covington Catholic student Nick Sandmann." *The Washington Times.* Accessed July 23, 2020. https://www.washingtontimes.com/news/2020/jan/7/cnn-settles-275m-lawsuit-covington-catholic-studen/.

up information to the contrary is spreading dangerous lies and must be silenced. Of course, this is their interpretation of what is true and false or their interpretation of a particular message even if that interpretation is highly subjective. These days, they often claim these interpretations are based on evidence or what they call "fact checks." Of course, the "evidence" or "facts" that they choose are often highly selective and come from questionable sources or from the prevailing scientific or academic thought—and we know what is considered absolute truth in the past (like the earth is flat) can reverse position over time (like Cleopatra and that snake). So, it is irrelevant if you think vaccines are necessary to public health or you think they are possibly damaging to the individual or you are in neither camp. What is frightening is that all opinions and discussions may not be permitted to reach the greater public and that someone behind the curtain can control what information you can access and evaluate for yourself.

Consider this: When Twitter first "fact-checked" a tweet of President Trump, Twitter found President Trump's opinion to be misleading with regards to the potential fraud that could be committed with mail balloting. Voter fraud is one of those issues that rational people know does occur, yet the Left vehemently claims it doesn't. We know why, of course; it is one of their favorite ways to swing an election! How many stories have we heard of newly "discovered" ballot boxes in the back of some trunk in south Florida that are inexplicably full of Democrat ballots when the tally is neck and neck? Just recently, in the 2018 midterms at the end of election night, seven California Republicans were ahead in their races. Over the next several hours, as provisional and absentee ballots were counted, *all* seven races swung in favor of Democrats, helping usher in a

Democrat majority in the national Congress. Well, we shouldn't have been surprised. California legalized ballot harvesting where volunteers can go door to door with ballots and "help" people cast their votes.[5] Who ensures that the ballot is filled out by the correct person? Who makes sure all the ballots, and not just the ones that they want, make it back to the precinct? It becomes quite obvious there is potential for fraud, and with mail-in balloting done at the national level, the possibilities are limitless for the most ruthless players.

But Twitter disagreed and "fact-checked" his tweets. Their supporting documents? Articles from *The Washington Post* and CNN. Hilarious. Now, what about this claim from the world of platforms and censoring: that President Trump was encouraging violence when he stated, "When the looting starts, the shooting starts" during the George Floyd protests of 2020? Of course, this was a very liberal interpretation, and by that, I mean an interpretation by leftists running these platforms. It was pretty clear that what President Trump was actually saying was when people loot, storekeepers and restaurant owners may turn to protecting their own places by shooting down these criminals. But, okay, let's misconstrue that comment and then block President Trump's words from these platforms. Is this acceptable? Are platforms like bookstores, where the overlords can choose what goes out to the public? Or because media platforms are so massive and open to the public in the style of a worldwide forum, should they have no right to choose who gets to speak and who does not and no right to censor what is being said? And, then, if they allow false information to purposely be distributed to the public,

---

5.   Marinucci, Carla. "GOP Cries Foul after California Thumping." POLITICO. Last modified November 30, 2018. https://www.politico.com/story/2018/11/29/california-2018-midterm-elections-results-voting-republicans-1031072.

are they really publishers who should then have the right to be sued? Is censoring information and, at the same time, choosing information nothing like being a bookstore and more like being a publisher? When President Trump fought back and wanted to make social media platforms publishers who could be sued for libel, was he protecting free speech or preventing it? It is very complicated, and in a world where just a few massive companies control what is disseminated to the public, it is hard to make a choice that is backfire-proof.

PAT

In case readers find it confusing as to what the issue between a platform and a publisher is, I can offer a clear example. When I wrote my book, *Profile of the Disappearance of Madeleine McCann* in 2011 based on the disappearance of a three-year-old British girl from the vacation flat her family rented in Portugal in 2007, I could not find a publisher for the book. Madeleine McCann's parents are very litigious, so even though I very carefully couched my words in the book, no accusations were made of anyone's guilt, and everything was a theory based on evidence, publishers still didn't want to risk a potential legal battle. So, I self-published it on Amazon. The book started selling like gangbusters and was positioned right under the book written by Madeleine McCann's mother. Five weeks went by, the reviews were great, and then the book vanished.

I wrote to Amazon asking what had happened. Where was my book? Amazon told me they had been threatened with a lawsuit by the McCanns for libel and pulled the book. After that, Twitter supporters of the book went crazy, accusing Amazon of censorship, sending me their sympathies, and asking how pissed I was at Amazon. I told them I understood exactly why Amazon did what they did and that, if I were them, I would have done the same! My fans were shocked! What? How could this be?

Well, I understood the problem. When my other books had been published by traditional book publishers, they went into brick-and-mortar stores and Amazon as items for sale, a market for books. The bookstore is not responsible for the material in the books (unless it is child pornography as it is illegal), and if someone doesn't like what is in the book, thinks it is libelous, they sue the publisher and the author, not the bookstore.

But when Amazon started allowing authors to self-publish via their own platform, they, for all intents and purposes, became a publisher when they provided the methodology to develop and print the book (in Kindle or paper form); the minute Amazon hit the button and allowed the book to go public on their site, they became a publisher and liable for what was in the book. Therefore, they *were* the publisher of my book, and they pulled it quickly so they wouldn't be embroiled in a lawsuit. My book was doing well, but it wasn't making them a million dollars, in which case the legal costs would have been well-worth it (as I believe Amazon would have won the case).

So, now we have this similar issue with content on the internet. Who gets to decide what will be published on Facebook and Twitter and on Google? Who gets to decide how algorithms work so that some content gets to be seen by millions and other content only gets seen by a few? Who gets to decide what news shows up first or at all on a Google search? How will these choices allow for free speech if so much of our speech online is being gagged? I don't know how this will all turn out, but it is a very concerning issue as liberals seem to be in control of our internet access and conservatives risk having their voices silenced forever.

CHAPTER SIX

FAKE NEWS, FAKE HATE CRIMES, AND THE LOSS OF DUE PROCESS

"It may be true that the law cannot make a man love me, but it can keep him from lynching me, and I think that's pretty important."

MARTIN LUTHER KING, JR.[1]

The concept of innocent until proven guilty used to be one of the defining differences between our country and many others in the world. Along with this concept was the idea of a timely accusation, that a citizen has the right—or at least he should—to provide a defense, and accusations made years later deny the defendant the ability to provide evidence to support his innocence and to prove his accuser is making a false claim. If years pass, witnesses die, memories vanish, paperwork proving times and places no longer exist, and then the entire case comes down to a "she said, he said" debacle. The jury or the Congress

1.   Mindock, Clark. "Martin Luther King Jr: 50 quotes from the civil rights leader who inspired a nation." *Independent*. Last modified January 20, 2020. https://www.independent.co.uk/news/world/americas/martin-luther-king-quotes-death-assassination-mlk-jr-a8855071.html.

or the public or whomever the accused is being paraded in front of often has a mindset of perceived guilt of one of the parties. We can see this in the push to #believeher, as if all women are to be believed in spite of questionable statements and lack of supporting evidence. That Supreme Court Justice Brett Kavanaugh was dragged through a complete circus in front of the entire nation, accused of a sexual assault with zero evidence that such an incident even occurred, is one of the most extreme examples of how due process is being squashed in order to promote agendas. Where people used to exercise caution when it came to people making claims about the behaviors of others, now it has become all too commonplace as a strategy in a race war, sex war, or political war. #MeToo and #racism became hashtags for a multitude of stories that have gone viral on YouTube or on Twitter, some making it into the mainstream media or the courts. If the story was useful, evidence was not that necessary.

PAT

During the accusations made against Bill Cosby by the #MeToo brigade, I tested the theory that agenda was far more important than evidence. I wasn't trying to prove him to be innocent; I was aiming to help people understand the rush to judgment based on claims prior to evidence actually being presented in court. I tossed up a blog post that I created in all of fifteen minutes and asked readers if they believed that I had indeed been assaulted by Tommy Chong (of Cheech and Chong fame) when I was an extra in Hollywood over forty years ago. I thought that it would be clear that this was a challenge to think about the problem of questionable allegations, but within minutes of posting the blog, I received many emails and comments sending me hugs and sympathy for having had to survive such a terrible experience. Then I got a phone call from a prominent lawyer who I did television news shows with, and he offered to take my case against Tommy Chong to court! Here is the post that was complete fantasy and yet, to my horror, very convincing to the readers. And after reading this, one must ask: Isn't it possible that Dr. Blasey Ford made up a story just like this although some thought it was "too real" to be a fake?

Did Tommy Chong Sexually Assault Criminal Profiler Pat Brown?

True or false? Should you believe this and should the media run with it?[2]

When I was 19 years old, I wished to become an actress in Hollywood. One day, on the set of Cheech and Chong, I was asked to stand in for an actress who was getting her hair done. I was told to lie on the bed with Tommy Chong, with the sheets and duvet covering us both, my side of the covers pulled over my face so that during filming it would not be noticed that I was body doubling for the actress.

While under the covers with Chong, I felt his hand cup my breast and then travel down my body to feel between my legs. He grabbed my hand and placed it on his penis and rubbed it up and down. I was mortified and didn't know what to do because the camera was rolling and there were people all around. I was only nineteen and naive and not very versed in how to deal with sexual assault, a sexual assault that was occurring with a group of men surrounding the bed, a group of

2.	Brown, Pat. "Did Tommy Chong Sexually Assault Criminal Profiler Pat Brown?" *The Daily Profiler*. Accessed July 18 2020. https://patbrownprofiling.blogspot. com/2016/10/did-tommy-chong-sexual-assault-criminal_88.html.

men who were friends with Mr. Chong, a famous actor and comedian, and me, a nobody that they could care less about.

I remained paralyzed under the sheet while Chong laughed with his crew and continued to move his hands and mine wherever he wanted. When they finished filming and the actress I was standing in for came into the room, I was summarily dismissed and I got out of the bed and pulled my dress down in front of everyone; I was crying but no one even looked at me and I ran from the room.

I was so traumatized by the experience that I left Hollywood and my dreams and over the years I had to seek counseling as I didn't trust men after that. I only told my sister and father what happened because they asked why I left Hollywood so abruptly and gave up on my long desired acting career.

I didn't come forward years ago because I was just an extra in the film industry and I knew no one would believe me over Tommy Chong who was loved and admired by many. But, now that I, too, have been on television for years and I am more mature and able to handle the fallout, I want to come forward and let people, especially other women who may have been abused by Mr. Chong, to know what happened to me and encourage others to come forward if they have had a similar experience. I want to let the public know that no one should get away with sexual assault just because they are famous and the victim is not. I hope coming forward will help others deal with sexual abuse and bring their abusers to justice.

Now, to the evidence:

On the side of Pat Brown:

She can prove she was in Hollywood at the time she claims the incident occurred.

She can prove by way of old dated letters (with the envelope) that she was on the set of Cheech and Chong's movie.

Her sister will verify that she was told by Pat Brown that the incident occurred and that she was told of the incident shortly after it occurred.

On the side of Tommy Chong:

No one remembers Pat Brown on the set while the movie was being filmed.

No one remembers an incident in which Tommy Chong was in the bed with Pat Brown.

No one remembers an incident in which an upset young extra jumped from the bed with her dress up over her waist and ran crying from the room.

The father of Pat Brown is dead; therefore, he cannot testify to what she said years ago.

Even if Pat Brown claimed years ago Tommy Chong sexually assaulted her, there is no way of knowing if this was truthful or just a fantastical claim of Pat Brown's to gain attention or to explain to her family her failure in Hollywood as an actress.

No one knows if Pat Brown and her sister are telling this story in order to achieve notoriety or money.

If other women come forward with similar claims, do you believe this adds to the evidence on Pat Brown's side of the equation?

Do you think this is a story the media should spread and a case Gloria Allred should take up since no police report was ever filed?

If this story goes public, who do you think the victim is? Pat Brown or Tommy Chong?

DISCLAIMER: I have just received a phone call offering me legal representation against Tommy Chong. THE POST IS FICTION! It is meant to make people THINK TWICE about media stories in which a famous person is accused of sexual assault without proof. I was NOT assaulted by Tommy Chong or any other famous person.

Criminal Profiler Pat Brown
October 16, 2016

DAVE

Rather frightening, isn't it? Where is the due process when stories are told of something that supposedly happened decades ago and there is nothing to verify whether the story is true or not? Is this a new version of public lynching? Where blacks once were hung without due process based on the story of one white woman, are we now destroying people's lives because they are men, white men, conservatives, blacks who don't conform, women who aren't feminist or feminist enough, whatever group the Left decides to attempt to destroy? That Justice Kavanaugh was even made to go through that atrocity of a fake trial is a testament to how far we have lowered our standards of fairness and the application of the law equally to all people.

One of the most egregious examples of guilty until proven innocent is the Trump/Russia collusion hoax. At the time of this writing, we know it was just that, a hoax. Robert Mueller's 400-page report not only cleared Trump and his campaign of colluding with the Russian government but noted that members of his campaign rejected offers from Russian government-linked persons. Astonishingly, though, there are those who still believe there was collusion. To be fair, some of these people are the most disingenuous politicians ever to slither through the halls of Congress, but there are others who honestly believe it did occur. That is perhaps the most troubling aspect. Once a lie is repeated often enough, even exculpatory information fails to change the minds of certain individuals. That is the power of lies, and this highlights the danger that fake news presents to our republic.

The term "Fake News" was not invented by President Trump, but he certainly has taken ownership of the phrase. And why shouldn't he? More so than any president before him, he has been the victim of one fake news story after another from purported "papers of record." How many news stories did *The New York Times* and *Washington Post* write about a Trump/Russia collusion? They are too numerous to count. But an important distinction must be made: there is irresponsible journalism where a reporter might put out a story that has dubious sources in an effort to gain prominence in the news industry, and then there are reporters and news outlets actively participating in the perpetuation of a false narrative in order to achieve an objective. In the case of President Trump, they sought his impeachment and removal from office. This behavior by the media is much more than just irresponsible journalism; it is outright participation in an effort to reverse an election. Who again is a threat to "democracy?" And if the press thinks Donald Trump's bemoaning of fake news is a threat to democracy, perhaps they should read about the actions undertaken by

Abraham Lincoln during the Civil War. Lincoln, in fact, shut down hundreds of newspapers that were sympathetic to the rebel cause. This is not a defense of his actions but rather an attempt to give context. Trump has not closed any newspapers, shut down any cable news network, or prevented any journalist from writing or saying anything. Free speech is alive and well despite what the court jesters on CNN claim.

How do we fight back against fake news? Shut down newspapers like Lincoln? Eavesdrop on journalists like the Obama administration? No, and as Americans who truly believe in free speech, we do not support authoritarian actions to silence our enemies. The solution is always the same: speak out against the frauds in the media, turn off the stations that spew garbage, and support politicians who are willing to fight back. There is no magic wand to wave, and we should not behave like the people on the Left who use intimidation and violence to achieve their objectives. The silent majority cannot remain silent. This will be a theme in this book. Every day the demographics of this country work against us, as do our destructive open-borders policy, and time is running out. Quiet dissent is no longer an option.

PAT

Some people think that we are exaggerating the news media to be heavily to the left and pushing an agenda rather than factual information. I remember being in the green room of MSNBC a couple of years ago, and the room was infested with journalists and guests ranting about President Trump and what a horrible man he was. It was extremely uncomfortable sitting there listening to all this garbage; everyone was speaking as if what they were saying was 100 percent the truth about President

Trump and surely not one person in the room would disagree with what was being said. After all, this was not Fox! Wow. If you don't think the media is biased as all get out, have a seat in the green rooms of the majority of the news stations.

As Chris Plante on his WMAL show often says, "The incredibly corrupt and dishonest Democrat Party and the Mainstream Media…but I repeat myself…."[3]

How did we get here?

Fake news is certainly not new. "Yellow journalism" has been around for a great deal of history, and the term was coined in the 1890s when a circulation war erupted between William Randolph Hearst's *New York Journal* and Joseph Pulitzer's *New York World.*[4] So nothing new under the sun. But since the election of Donald Trump in 2016, there seems to be no limit to the level fake news has risen.

But let's look at the Wikipedia definition, which I think is quite good.

> Yellow Journalism or the Yellow Press are American terms for journalism and associated newspapers that present little or no legitimate well-researched news while instead using eye-catching headlines for increased sales. Techniques may include exaggerations of news events, scandal-mongering, or sensationalism. By extension, the term yellow journalism is used today as a pejorative to decry any journalism that treats news in an unprofessional or unethical fashion.[5]

3.   Allnatt, Chris. "The Chris Plante Show." YouTube. March 18, 2020. Video, 138 min. https://youtu.be/WaG_Jr2fIB8.

4.   "Yellow Journalism." Wikipedia. Last modified July 31, 2020. https://en.wikipedia.org/wiki/Yellow_journalism.

5.   "Yellow Journalism." Wikipedia. Last modified July 31, 2020. https://en.wikipedia.org/wiki/Yellow_journalism.

It is bad enough that yellow journalism of the sensation-alizing type exists, à la the *Network* movie depiction. Where it is most concerning is when agenda, even more than ratings, lies behind the lies that are presented as facts and truth, lies intending to sway the public's viewpoint of a particular issue. Lies not only harm the general public, the citizenry, but also individuals and families who lack the means to fight back against so huge an organization. There may be no way to get a noticeable retraction or to be able to sue such an organiza-tion, so such a media corporation has pretty much a playing field advantage in saying whatever they please without any negative consequences. Here are a few examples of damage done to my own family and to me and my own reputation. First, a strange story from almost a century ago now, one that only recently was I able to determine what was true and what was not.

My father, who died some seven years ago, liked to tell me a bit about the family tree. He told me of a woman writer a couple of generations back who he thought I took after. He told me of a female doctor in the family who died in Auschwitz. And then he told this strange story with salt-and-pepper shakers, of which I remember little except that he took the pepper shaker (I suppose representing a black sheep of the family, nothing racial) and shoved it across the table and said, "That woman! That actress!" But when I asked my father to elaborate, he abruptly changed the subject. I never had a clue as to who this horrible woman was supposed to be, but she clearly upset him, and my father was not one who got upset easily.

Fast-forward to around 2014. My second cousin wrote to my sisters and me (upon hearing of both my father's and my mother's deaths) and, along with her condolences, asked if we wished to exchange information about our ancestry, perhaps more about my grandfather Leo and our famous great-great uncle, Leopold Sonnemann, publisher of the *Frankfurter Zeitung* and a champion for Jewish rights and social and monetary reform. Oh, and maybe more about *that woman* that she had heard about from her father whose name he never told her but that clearly bothered him.

So, this email inspired me to toss a few search terms into Google, and there it was, the myth that had dogged my father and our German relatives all their lives:

Emmy Göring, actress and wife of Hermann Göring—who not only was a top dog Nazi but a major thief of European art (watch the movie *Monument Men*)—was said to be the great niece of the famous publisher, Leopold Sonnemann, which would make her my great aunt. Oh. My. God. Yikes!

Now it made sense why my father was so upset about *that* woman. He didn't want his family name linked to Emmy Göring. After all, he had a top-secret clearance and worked for the Department of Defense. He must have worried that someone might trace our family history back to the Nazi party and all the infamy of the convicted war criminal Herman Göring and of Adolf Hitler, who was best man at Hermann and Emmy's wedding.

He and my cousin's father weren't the only ones in the family with this suspicion; I found out from my cousin that one of our Italian relatives had also commented on "that horrible woman" being on our family tree!

But, then again, maybe she wasn't on our tree at all.

Some journalists of yesteryear seem to be just as ethically challenged (anything that makes a good story) and were as careless as many of our news reporters of today. Here is what appears to have happened: one journalist from the *New York Post* wrote a story that claimed Emmy Göring née Sonnemann was Jewish and the grand-niece of Leopold Sonnemann and that her father was August Sonnemann, my father's grandfather. Then another paper, denying this story to be true, claimed that the first journalist had erred in connecting her to my family because Emmy Sonnemann's father was a different August Sonnemann. But it turns out, as far as I and my cousin have researched, that Emmy Göring's father was not an August at all nor was her father Jewish nor can I find her anywhere on the family tree in our research! So, unless Hermann Göring really doctored up some good paperwork and our family managed to eliminate all traces of a black sheep, these 1935 journalists published stories without doing proper research or presenting any proof. The stories were good enough, though, to stir up a lot of gossip around the time of Emmy Sonnemann's wedding to Hermann and served as a rather unnerving rumor that eventually affected my father and other relatives even though they should have had firsthand (or at least secondhand) information that would contradict these erroneous reports. But this goes to prove the power the press has upon people; there is a strange tendency for people to believe what they read even if it flies in the face of known facts or just seems to come out of nowhere. If a story is in a major newspaper, the journalist must be telling the truth or the editor wouldn't allow it to be published. Even I was taken aback by the story of my possible connection to Emmy Göring and will probably research more still to be sure I am not missing something—even though there seems to be no basis for the claim at all.

So I say to everyone: Don't just believe what you read in the paper; be sure there is evidence to back up any and all claims. Or, like my father, you just might spend a lifetime hiding a "fact" that never really was one.

Now, let me fast-forward to a few years ago. I have been a longtime commenter on the famous Madeleine McCann case, the mystery surrounding the three-year-old British girl who disappeared from her parent's vacation flat in Portugal in the spring of 2007, never to be seen again. As I stated earlier, I wrote a book on the case, *Profile of the Disappearance of Madeleine McCann,* which I self-published on Amazon because no publisher wanted to take the chance of getting sued by Kate and Gerry McCann, the parents of the little girl. They had already sued Gonçalo Amaral, the Portuguese detective who wrote a book on the case in Portuguese, *The Truth of the Lie,* which sold like hotcakes in his native country. The book was pulled from that market, and the case had to go all the way the Supreme Court of Portugal before Mr. Amaral won on the appeals and the book went back on the market (but not before destroying him financially).

In my book on the case, I agreed with Mr. Gonçalo's theory that there was no evidence of an abduction and that the little girl likely died an accidental death by way of an overdose of medication and a fall from a couch, ending up behind it on the floor and suffering positional asphyxiation (which I supported with a good deal of evidence and crime scene and behavioral analysis). Although I clearly stated that my analysis was a theory and not accusation of guilt, the parents sent their top libel lawyers, Carter-Ruck, to threaten Amazon with a libel suit. Amazon pulled the book to be on the safe side, but the book is still for sale at Smashwords and Barnes & Noble because those online bookstores don't sell but a small portion of what Amazon sells. I guess the McCanns didn't want to waste their time with lesser fish.

At any rate, I became the second-most go-to person on the Madeleine McCann case after Gonçalo Amaral (and I spoke English where he did not), so I did many an interview and show about the case early on, before any dissent from the abduction story became such a liability. In the last ten years, I have rarely done any more TV interviews on the case, but in 2017, I agreed to do one for Australian television. What a nightmare! I fought back against what these "news" people did to me, and this came out in the UK paper *The Sun* in April of 2017.[6]

'THEY ANNIHILATED ME' Madeleine McCann crime expert who told doc her parents Gerry and Kate may have hidden body plans to sue show for twisting her comments

Criminal profiler says her views on Maddie's disappearance were misrepresented.

A CRIME expert who told an explosive documentary that Kate and Gerry McCann could have hidden their daughter Madeleine's body plans to SUE the Aussie TV channel which ran the show.

US criminal profiler Pat Brown featured on Channel 7's Sunday Night show claiming the McCanns could have put Maddie's body in a bag, hid it at the beach and moved it weeks later.

But the expert – who told the show there was a possibility Madeleine had been killed as the result of an

6.   Baker, Neal, and Tui Benjiman. "They Annihilated Me." *The Sun*. Last modified April 24, 2017. https://www.thesun.co.uk/news/3401813/madeleine-mccann-crime-expert-who-told-doc-her-parents-gerry-and-kate-may-have-hidden-body-plans-to-sue-show-for-twisting-her-comments/.

accident, neglect or abuse – now plans to sue for defamation as although she said it was possible, she never said the McCanns did it.

Pat claims in her original hour-long Skype interview with journalist Rahni Sadler that she made it clear this was only a theory based on her view of the evidence available.

Pat, who said she has received hate mail since the show aired, revealed: "I thought whether people agreed with the evidence or not, I would be able to present this as a professional.

"I never stated the McCanns were guilty of anything other than neglecting their children, and I will stand by that.

"I never said the McCanns are guilty of covering up the death of their child or moving their child's body.

"The show purposefully set out to destroy my reputation. The only reason I was featured was to annihilate me by making me look foolish."

Pat's lawyer Brian Close said he had identified multiple misrepresentation, false light and defamation claims against Seven West Media and Rahni Sadler.

He said: "The misleading edits portray Pat Brown in a false light by contorting her statements and changing their substance, and the broadcasts and publications have done and continue to do damage to Ms. Brown's professional reputation wherever they are viewed around the world."

Seven News Media, which runs the channel, has been approached for comment.

On the programme, Pat said: "There are other cases where a child has come to some kind of harm by way of a parent either by neglect or abuse and the parents have indeed covered that crime up by trying to move the child's body and claim that the child has gone missing and has been abducted."

And in a trailer for the show, she was quoted as saying: "They are lying and they are concealing guilt."

Wow! That trailer floored me! It was an edit from a longer statement about parents whose children go missing or are found murdered, that there are instances when parents claim they have no knowledge of what happened to their child, but in reality "they are lying and they are concealing guilt." I never made a blatant statement that the McCanns were lying or were concealing guilt. That kind of statement would open me up to a lawsuit from the McCanns and, surely, after dealing with the McCanns' litigiousness for over a decade and having my own book pulled from the market, I knew enough to always talk about the case and the parents only in theories and what evidence supports those theories. But *Sunday Night* edited that statement to gain viewers for their show, and they put questions or scenarios before my answers that didn't exist during the interview, all in an effort to mock my profiling theory of Madeleine McCann's disappearance.

So why did I do the *Sunday Night* show?

I did the show because Australia had been the first country to allow me to present detailed case evidence instead of a few quick words about the generalities of missing children.

I did the show because I wanted the truth out there in the mainstream media, and this was a rare opportunity as talking about the facts of the case had been off-limits for over seven years.

I did the show because it was billed to me by Rahni Sadler as a public affairs show. I would not have done it if I knew the kind of show it really was. Now, some cannot believe that I didn't do my homework before doing the interview and that I did not have a contract that required them to allow me final say on the content. These folks do not understand the media industry. When there is breaking news, calls come in from print, radio, and television, one after the other. Half the time, I don't even remember who I talked to until I see a story come out. I *do* now refuse almost all print and taped radio and television because I don't like the editing and misquoting. I *do* still do documentary shows *for* money if I am being brought on as a valued expert, as in the documentary *The Unsolved Death of Cleopatra* or *Mystery Files: Jack the Ripper.* Until three years ago, all of my experiences up to then had been positive; I was *their* expert, and they wanted to make me look good, and they *wanted* my analysis to support the show. Since, then, after this awful *Sunday Night* experience, I went on to have another unpleasant experience with an Oxygen show on the Martha Moxley case. They, too, set me up to be the person with a ridiculous theory and the evidence I presented to support my theory was edited or left out. Since then, I will no longer do even documentaries without absolute proof I am not going to be screwed.

So, normally, when news media calls, we in the business rarely spend much time studying the show. We are going to do a straightforward question-and-answer session. When Rahni Sadler contacted me and stated she wanted my analysis for a public affairs show, I accepted and went down the street to a hotel where there was a film crew waiting. Rahni was in Australia, and we communicated through Skype. No paperwork was signed, as is usual with any news show (a documentary will have you sign an appearance agreement: a contract that is about money to be paid for one's participation and has nothing to do with having any say over the final production unless you are some huge star or Casey Anthony); no appearance agreement should have been necessary with this just being a straight public affairs news show with my words unedited and in full. The interview lasted approximately an hour, and Rahni and I did a continuous discussion, again like a news show. Documentaries usually have you repeat the question in your answer so they can insert it where it is needed (without the question before) and they often ask the question a number of times to make sure they have a good statement. Rahni did not do this. She went right through the questions, and I answered them. It is clear to me now that she was only looking for a few statements she could misconstrue to accomplish her mission of discrediting me and my analysis of the McCann case.

In all my history of television and work with programs, I had *never* encountered this kind of unethical behavior until this point in time. No producer until this show (and the subsequent Oxygen Channel's *Murder and Justice: The Case of Martha Moxley*) had ever duped me into doing a show that was going to humiliate me and no show has ever so twisted my statements and defamed me. After fifteen years in television, I had no expectation—even in the McCann case—to be so screwed over. But this is now, and this is important: in today's world, *many* shows, both news and documentaries cannot be trusted to be honorable. That is why I pretty much refuse all media unless I am absolutely sure the program or story is going to be factual and not agenda-driven behind my back.

So, what happened to the lawsuit, you wonder? Did I make a killing off it? No, I never even got to file it. Why? Because Australia has a ridiculous law that states if you don't lose income in Australia, you don't have grounds for a loss of income due to libel. Don't you think *Sunday Night* and *Channel 7* knew this when they brought on someone from *outside* their country? In other words, they could destroy my reputation and ruin my income in the United States and elsewhere because there would be no possibility of a lawsuit against them in Australia.

The only thing they didn't plan on was the really bad publicity they got when I went to the UK press. Wikipedia states (without reference to me), *"In April 2017, Sadler resigned from a full-time position at Seven but continues to work with the network on a freelance basis."[7]* So sad.

The Sun wasn't the only story who carried my saga with Rahni Sadler and *Sunday Night*; the story appeared in half a dozen UK publications. But it is a bit amusing that *The Sun* wrote a proper story of what happened in this case and then only a couple years later, *they* libeled me concerning the very same Madeleine McCann case! Although they didn't have me saying things that would get me sued by the McCanns, they completely misrepresented me by stating in a headline and elsewhere that I believed Madeleine McCann had been abducted, something I had never, ever said and have always said the opposite was most likely to be true! Where did they get these erroneous statements from? Well, they listened to a radio show I had done and then picked out some words, scrambled them around, and put them in their story. They never even interviewed me.

I fought back. I learned I would never be able to get through a lawsuit in England for libel against a media outlet, but that there was an oversight group that supposedly had some weight in keeping the media in line. Considering this group

---

7.   "Rahni Sadler." Wikipedia. Last modified August 1, 2020. https://en.wikipedia.org/wiki/Rahni_Sadler.

really seems to have no effect that I could note on the industry, I am not sure they are worth much. However, after months of fighting over a retraction and an apology and getting wording that wasn't just an easy way out with a simple correction, I got this rare half-baked apology from *The Sun*:

> Apology to criminal profiler Pat Brown
>
> An article "KEY TO FINDING MADDIE expert says mystery man spotted on night she disappeared is key to solving case of missing Madeleine McCann" (11 March) originally had a headline which reported that criminal profiler Pat Brown believed Madeleine McCann may have been abducted by a mystery man seen on the night she disappeared. To clarify, she believes that the man is key to solving the case, but does not believe he abducted Madeleine. A version of the headline also suggested that two 'mystery men' seen on the night may have been the same person; in fact, Pat Brown believes they were different men. We apologize for the error.[8]

Of course, did this apology appear on a prominent page of a new printed edition of *The Sun*? Of course not! It appeared in a correction section of the online version, which I am sure few saw. And did it include the fact that I do not believe that the evidence does not support an abduction? No, they still managed to skirt around that. And did they say they deliberately misrepresented what I said? No, it was just an "error."

Now you can understand why the media can get away with such appalling yellow journalism. There is little oversight, little

8. "Apology to criminal profiler Pat Brown." *The Sun*. Last modified July 19, 2019. https://www.thesun.co.uk/clarifications/9539250/apology-to-criminal-profiler-pat-brown/.

recourse for misrepresentation, and if our journalists don't police themselves, we can only depend on the public to turn the channel or turn off the television, to refuse to buy the newspaper, or to refrain from clicking on an online headline if it is from an untrustworthy news source. You, the public, may be our only army against the corrupt media.

DAVE

As I write this, Joe Biden is going through his own #MeToo moment. No, not for all the creepy touching we've seen him do on camera to women old and young alike, but for an incident that is alleged to have happened in 1992. Tara Reade, working for then Senator Joe Biden, claims that he sexually assaulted her in the Russell Senate Office Building. Did this attack occur? I have zero clue. Sometimes, when women are sexually assaulted, there may be a lack of evidence to provide for arrest or prosecution, or perhaps they were too scared to come forward when evidence could have been collected. But, as we have seen with the Duke lacrosse case, where members of the team were accused of sexual assault, or the case of Tawana Brawley who claimed four white men raped her, both cases turned out to be false accusations. This puts our society and men in a dilemma; if there is no direct evidence of an attack other than witness testimony, is that enough to condemn someone? Legally, men have been sent to jail for rape with the only evidence being the victim's testimony, and sometimes that accusation has turned out to be false or a case of mistaken identity. As a man in this society, it is unsettling. Yet when a story came out about Vice President Mike Pence's personal rules of conduct with women other than his wife, he was roundly mocked by many members of the mainstream media as being some weird Christian zealot.

To be honest, he is a bit more religious than I am, but I can't help but respect the decision he made. His rule: never be alone in room with a woman who is not his wife. One-on-one meetings or interviews with women are to be conducted in a common area, not in his hotel room or behind closed doors anywhere. Overly rigid? You might think so, but to this day, there has not been one accusation made against Mike Pence.

And now, more men are following Mike Pence's guidelines, which has had negative unintended consequences for women in the workplace. Men in positions of power now have to evaluate the risk of bringing along a young, attractive subordinate on a business trip. Or to take her out for lunch as a reward for hard work or to engage in mentoring in more informal environment. Why take the chance? Sexism is no longer the only issue that can hurt women; now it is self-preservation.

While a false accusation can destroy one's reputation, a government that takes away due process can destroy one's life and take one's freedom. I want to like the ACLU, even when they defend some reprehensible people and positions, because I find it of the utmost importance that we challenge the government's power to imprison its citizens. But then to my dismay, I see liberals more than excited to see the government over-reaching to get someone thrown in jail. In this case, three-star general Michael Flynn. Even when evidence arose that the FBI looked to entrap him in a scheme to get him fired or imprisoned, they still insisted that he was guilty and should be locked up. Aren't these the people that supposedly question government power? Were they not the same people who protested against J. Edgar Hoover's FBI in the '60s when they spied on Martin Luther King and gathered blackmail against politicians? Yet now they are on the side of the FBI even when the motives of the FBI became suspect. If the national security advisor to the president can be railroaded and thrown in prison, what can they do to you, a common citizen? You have no voice, no power, and you are probably not a multi-millionaire able to afford hundreds of thousands in legal fees. What recourse do you have? It is a scary thought, yet while the Left attacks the entirety of police and law enforcement, they, at the same time, support the use of law enforcement against their political enemies. A baffling contradiction.

PAT

Hey, Dave, before we end this discussion we can't forget about Jussie Smollett! He may be yesterday's news, but how the news media jumped on the story! They loved, loved, loved that some MAGA white supremacists had attacked a black man and a celebrity and hurled racial and homophobic slurs at him, poured some kind of chemical on him, and then hung a noose around his neck! Oh, the perfect hate crime! The news media was salivating! For a Trump-hating press, this was a delicious story. Instead of waiting for enough information to determine whether such an outrageous claim (and it was such a ridiculous story that you would think they would be wary, but then again, they so wanted it to be true they really didn't care to question it) had evidence to back it, they ran and ran and ran with outrage pouring out of commentator's mouths, how this was proof that MAGA people were racists and deplorables. They were unwilling to allow any due process or any investigation before they rushed to judgment.

Then came strong evidence that none of this was true and Jussie had staged a hate crime with the help of two Nigerian men. He got nailed with filing a false police report, but then the Cook County State's Attorney's Office dismissed the case three weeks later. Many months have passed with arguments and claims and counterclaims—more about the handling of the case than the actual crime—and much is still up in the air as to what charges should be levied and what other legal ethics matter should be dealt with .[9] But I ask this: Why wasn't he charged with a hate crime against white people? Because that was exactly what it was. He got off easy, and so did the media, who dropped the story like a hot potato. Did the media apologize for pushing this fake news? Of course not.

DAVE

We are led to believe the hate crimes against blacks are ubiquitous across the United States, yet upon further investigation, many of these hate crimes are completely fabricated. Jussie Smollett attacked by racist white Trump supporters in Chicago, a church in Mississippi the target of arson and racist graffiti, Jewish institutions receiving bomb threats. When these headlines pop up in local and national media, they paint a picture of a deeply racist nation with minorities frightened and apprehensive about threats to their well-being. Just one problem, the perpetrators of these reported crimes *were* minorities! Did the Jews in 1933 Germany have to fake hate crimes in order to bring attention their plight? How about African Americans in the deep south during the 1950s? Of course not. What these fake hate crimes are essentially is an admission that there aren't enough hate crimes occurring organically for liberal activists to latch on

9.   De Mar, Charlie. "Police Say Jussie Smollett Paid Two Men By Check To Stage
       Attack; 'This Publicity Stunt Was A Scar That Chicago Didn't Earn.'" CBS
       Chicago. Accessed July 18, 2020. https://chicago.cbslocal.com/2019/02/21/
       jussie-smollett-surrenders-disorderly-conduct-staged-attack/.

to and push a political agenda. Fake a hate crime, cash in on it, and move on before authorities get to the bottom of what really happened. What I find mind-boggling, though, is just how incompetent these bad actors are. Is it that hard to spray-paint Nazi graffiti on a wall without getting caught? Apparently so. Thankfully, their incompetence in faking hate crimes has alerted the public to their scam, and with the publicity given to the Smollett case, the public has a new level of skepticism.

CHAPTER SEVEN

MARXISM, RACISM, AND EDUCATION

"The Ultimate weakness of Communism is that it robs man of that quality which makes him man."

MARTIN LUTHER KING, JR.[1]

DAVE

When Barack Obama proclaimed during his 2008 presidential campaign that we needed "fundamental change," he encompassed the prevailing attitude of the progressive Left. America isn't fundamentally good with imperfections that need to be addressed, but fundamentally flawed from our founding days. To affect change at this scale, revolutionary thinking is required. The source for this in the capitalist West is Marxism and all its derivations. If you were to take an economics course in an American university, Marx would be studied in a rather narrow focus from a purely economic standpoint. To think of Marx simply in economic terms is shortsighted and missing out on his much larger impact. Marxism isn't simply an economic

---

1. "Martin Luther King Jr Takes on Communism." Our Florida Dream: Policy and Culture: . Accessed July 25, 2020. http://livingourfloridadream.com/public-policy-and-culture/martin-luther-king-jr-takes-on-communism/.

theory but a revolutionary attitude that is hostile toward traditional society.

The problem that Marx faced was, despite the flaws in capitalism, the capitalist system brought about the largest increase in the standard of living in the history of civilization and ushered in the rise of the middle class. How does one push for revolutionary change under these conditions? By creating instability and a victim class. By convincing enough people that traditional society intrinsically makes them second-class citizens, whether it be real or imagined. This line of thinking was perfected in the political philosophy known as *Critical Theory*. *Critical Theory* creates victim classes that altogether make a societal majority, which, in turn, creates a potent political force. Almost everyone except straight, white, Christian men could be considered part of the victim class. Women are subjugated beneath men, blacks beneath whites, gays beneath straights, Muslims beneath non-Muslims, and so on. These minority groups are then cobbled together to form a dysfunctional majority of unlikely bedfellows.

Out of *Critical Theory* comes an even more extreme philosophy, *Critical Race Theory*. This took the fight for equality one step further. While the civil rights movement aimed to bring about racial equality and equal opportunities for blacks, believers of *Critical Race Theory* would require the government to be responsible for uplifting or promoting the position of blacks in society regardless of their personal qualifications or the qualifications of others, their reasoning being that society is so steeped against the minority that, despite the best efforts of society and government, white privilege continues to put blacks at a disadvantage. Gone would be life, liberty, and the pursuit of happiness; instead, faceless bureaucrats will engineer society.

This thinking can be seen in a lower court ruling by current Supreme Court Justice Sonia Sotomayor, who ruled that whites could be discriminated against by the government in favor of minority candidates for certain public sector jobs. No longer would the most qualified candidate be selected, but the candidate that filled certain quotas. This attempt at righting historical social wrongs is unproductive in the long run. It not only lowers the expectations for certain individuals, but collectively lowers the quality of performance in critical public services. The adage goes that the road to hell is paved with good intentions, and if the more extreme voices of the progressive Left continue to gain power in our society, that road will become a short path to a dystopian future that none of will want to see.

Another dangerous concept is free education for all children in government schools; what a lovely idea with an underlying dangerous agenda.

There are certain segments of our society that progressives gravitate to, and none more than the education system. We are all familiar with the current atmosphere on college campuses, which are steadily becoming more authoritarian and radical in their thinking. Unfortunately, over the past several years, this radicalism is not only present on college campuses but has begun to take root in high schools and primary schools as well. Schools are no longer viewed by progressives as an institution of learning, but also a venue to promote social change, aka indoctrination. Make no mistake about it: social change is a fancy way of saying political agenda, and the sooner that political agenda can be pushed on your kids, the more likely it is to take hold. This progression of politics in the classroom has accelerated over the last decade. Topics that were considered complex issues to be disseminated by adults like transgenderism have manifested themselves in children's books read to kids as young as four and five. Sexual and gender ambiguity have become so prevalent and accepted among children that a network morning show, *Regis and Kelly*, proudly presented the brave story of a drag queen ten-year-old. And if your kid isn't a drag queen, your local school may invite one to read to them. What relevance this has to basic education is baffling, especially if one still has the antiquated view that school is strictly for basic learning, not social movement.

While progressives will deny it, this infiltration of radicalism into the curriculum has its roots in Marx and Engels. One such organization that spearheads this effort is Teaching for Change, an organization that encourages and trains teachers to "build" social justice in the classroom. In their mission statement, they say they are striving to build a more "equitable, multicultural society of global citizens," a statement filled with all the key buzzwords of the Left. The inspiration for their project is historian Howard Zinn, who, in reference to himself, said that he was "something of a Marxist." He is most famous for his book *A People's History of America*, which orates an alternative viewpoint of American history, much of it critical of the United States, specifically the government and our capitalist society. I do find his viewpoint to be interesting. As we have discovered, history is often the collective viewpoint of those in power, but should the mistakes of the past be used to destroy what we currently have? That seems to be the goal, yet progressives become upset when prominent conservatives suggest that they do not like America and want to fundamentally change it. Even the most superficial review of their material shows this in spades.

The importance of classroom activism to progressives cannot be overstated. Societal transformation doesn't happen organically; there are forces, often unseen, directing them from the shadows. Many events in history that, on the surface, had the appearance of occurring organically did, in fact, arise out of carefully constructed line of events. One of those well-known and much debated events was the "uprising" in Libya that led to the overrun of the American embassy. In an embarrassing sequence, the Obama administration first blamed a video posted on YouTube for inciting the violence, a claim that was farfetched from the beginning. Only later was it acknowledged that the Libyan uprising was, in fact, a coordinated event, planned to coincide with the anniversary of 9/11. Finding the real motive behind an action is like peeling an onion: behind every layer is another layer that only serves to obfuscate the issue.

The Left is an expert at this. Many of their groups have names that seem straightforward and innocuous. "Black Lives Matter," which arose during the Obama administration, is not an inflammatory name, yet digging deeper into their organization, I find their motives are far beyond preventing unjustified police violence against minorities. An even more ridiculous organization is Antifa—short for Anti-Fascism, a message they spread by committing acts of what I would call fascism. They aren't really promoting anti-violence; crack their outer shell, and you'll find pervasive amounts of Marxist ideology. Just as these groups do not advertise who they really are, the individuals that comprise them balk at being called Marxists. One leftover from the cold war is the repulsion Americans feel toward anyone labeled a communist or a Marxist. So, what does one do? Deny, deny, deny.

The tactics of Marxism are nothing new. Trotsky and Lenin explained their methods in detail in their many writings. Much of their focus, of course, was the Russian revolution and how to implement it. Two things stand out.

The first lesson to be learned is that honesty is not always the best course of action. While Marx and Engels pushed their revolutionary ideas from the perspective of their native Germany (which was quickly industrializing within its borders), Russia, on the other hand, had a large agrarian population that lived outside the urban centers, sprawled across a vast area. Many of these farmers were uneducated and unaware of the political inner workings of the Marxist revolutionaries. These were hardworking, simple folk who struggled enormously for the little they did have. After years of back-breaking work, some of them managed to purchase their own blocks of land. This was of concern to the revolutionaries. How do you convince these people to give up the private land they worked so hard for in favor of public ownership? The answer, according to Trotsky, is that you don't. In his writings, he acknowledged the necessity to conceal their real motives from certain segments of the population or suffer defeat. The lessons have been well-learned by many of the intellectuals who followed. Being open about Marxism and the endgame is unwise, especially in wealthy countries with a large middle class. Better to promote ideas that move toward Marxism rather than the outright pursuit of some of Marxism's more radical ideas, such as the confiscation of private property.

The second lesson to be learned is that the revolution is ongoing. The actual application for late-nineteenth and early-twentieth century Marxists was a strategy for capitalist societies they believed had reached a tipping point. But for those living in the present day, the strategy is for Marxists to chip away at society and transform it over time. We can then see the need to infiltrate the education system as early as possible. Adults are fairly fixed in their opinions, and it is difficult to get them to accept radically different ideas. In fact, over time, there is the tendency to for people become more conservative and less idealistic as the realities of life and survival become more acute. Wisely, Marx, in his tenth plank of his manifesto, advocated public education of children provided free by the government. This was not motivated by benevolence. Marx understood that, in order to transform society, the process of indoctrination must start as early in life as possible. This becomes clearer when we examine other works specifically by Engels. In *The Principles of Communism*, Engels advocated children to be raised in communes. In his mind, the relationship between child and parent was an institution of slavery. The public education system serves to further the goals of progressivism. And progressives, knowing that this is where children learn to accept socialist ideas, become quite aggressive in their disdain for private schools and homeschooling as these are places where they do not control the curriculum.

Looking at our education system today, with the knowledge of how Marx and Engels viewed individualism, the motivations of those on the Left come into focus. The Left pushes for social change, they push for free schooling for kids at a younger and younger age, after-school programs that keep children later and later into the day, and summer programs to fill in the gap between the school years. They can't take your kids from you like Engels wanted, but they can keep them away from you and in care of the system for as long as possible.

Think to yourself, who has had a bigger role in shaping your child's life: you or the State?

PAT

Just check out what Melissa Harris Perry of MSNBC said in April of 2019:

"We have to break through our private idea that kids belong to their parents or that kids belong to their families and recognize that kids belong to whole communities." [2]

Really? I think if God wanted parents to have no control over their children, we would lay eggs like frogs.

Leftists have worked to remove parental control from children's lives in various ways; they try to criminalize home birth, they want vaccinations to be mandatory from the minute a child enters the world, and they want, absolutely want, control over all education of children (and they want control over that education earlier and earlier) because that is where the most indoctrination can occur.

When I first started homeschooling in the 1980s, it was still a rather rare concept in the United States. Since leftists have not found a way to ban private schools (I am sure a good number of leftists would like to see this because, after all, private schools often have religious instruction interwoven into the curriculum), homeschooling became their target as it has become a popular choice of alternative education.

As Harvard professor Elizabeth Bartholet describes in 2019 in *The Arizona Law Review*:

2. Corkery, Marie Rose. "Conservatives counter 'hostility' of Harvard's 'anti-homeschool' event." Campus Reform. Accessed July 18, 2020. https://www.campusreform.org/?ID=14778.

It is [a] rapidly growing homeschooling phenomenon and the threat it poses to children and society. Homeschooling activists have in recent decades largely succeeded in their deregulation campaign, overwhelming legislators with aggressive advocacy. As a result, parents can now keep their children at home in the name of homeschooling free from any real scrutiny as to whether or how they are educating their children. Many homeschool because they want to isolate their children from ideas and values central to our democracy, determined to keep their children from exposure to views that might enable autonomous choice about their future lives. Many promote racial segregation and female subservience. Many question science. Abusive parents can keep their children at home free from the risk that teachers will report them to child protection services. Some homeschool precisely for this reason. This Article calls for a radical transformation in the homeschooling regime and a related rethinking of child rights. It recommends a presumptive ban on homeschooling, with the burden on parents to demonstrate justification for permission to homeschool.[3]

You will notice that missing from Bartholet's major concerns about homeschooling is any actual mention of reading, writing, and arithmetic. There is no worry of children failing to learn the basics of subjects like history, geography, science, literature, and so on. What she really is upset about is that not all

---

3.   Bartholet, Elizabeth. "HOMESCHOOLING: PARENT RIGHTS ABSOLUTISM VS. CHILD RIGHTS TO EDUCATION & PROTECTION." Arizona Law Review. Accessed July 18, 2020. https://arizonalawreview.org/pdf/62-1/62arizlrev1.pdf.

children will be subject to the "ideas and values central to our democracy" and they might not have "exposure to views that might enable autonomous choice about their future lives." If you read further in her article, she mentions what those "ideas and values" are that she fears children will miss out on if they are educated at home.

> A very large proportion of homeschooling parents are ideologically committed to isolating their children from the majority culture and indoctrinating them in views and values that are in serious conflict with that culture. Some believe that women should be subservient to men; others believe that race stamps some people as inferior to others. Many don't believe in the scientific method, looking to the Bible instead as their source for understanding the world....(they want to protect their children from) secularism, atheism, feminism and value relativism.[4]

To be sure, Bartholet throws in extreme examples of children who did not attend school who are abused, neglected, or in some very bizarre religious cult. That most homeschoolers are caring parents matters little to Bartholet because she believes that the state should be involved in the raising of our children as early and as thoroughly as possible. Why? Because she wants to be sure the leftists of the public school systems can teach their version of "ideas and values" central to their idea of our "democracy." Considering some public schools these days refuse to hang a photo of President Trump in the lobby but

---

4.   Bartholet, Elizabeth. "HOMESCHOOLING: PARENT RIGHTS ABSOLUTISM VS. CHILD RIGHTS TO EDUCATION & PROTECTION." *Arizona Law Review*. Accessed July 18, 2020. https://arizonalawreview.org/pdf/62-1/62arizlrev1.pdf.

have President Obama's photo front and center, we can have a pretty good idea of what ideas and values are going to be taught.

It was very clear when I homeschooled my children exactly what their concerns were as to my teaching my own kids. Every year, they would come to my house, usually two middle-aged ladies, and we would be required to let them in to evaluate our school program. Mind you, they were not there very long; they quite quickly shuffled through some of the children's work, asked a few questions about interacting with other children and playing sports. But mostly, they wanted to be sure we weren't keeping our kids away from children of other races. When they came into my house, they saw two biracial children and one black child and they immediately lost interest in their mission. We always got a quick okay, and they were out the door.

However, the families in our homeschool community, who happened to be all white, would call us up in a panic the day before and ask us to please come and visit them and be at their home prior to the time the two public school ladies would arrive! And we would help them out so when those ladies knocked on the door and came in the house, they would see the family's white children nicely playing with three nonwhite kids. And the family got their passing grade for properly socializing their children with other races.

I always wondered if those two ladies ever noticed that those same three nonwhite children were always there playing with each one of the white families they visited!

Our school systems are becoming more Marxist by the day. As Dave pointed out, strange bedfellows can be made of all the supposed victim classes if the agenda is to get rid of capitalism and institute a communist system in its place. If you think this is farfetched, just read through the *13 Guiding Principles*[5] of the Black Lives Matter curriculum for Black History Month that was instituted—yes, *instituted*—by the Prince George's County School Board in Maryland in 2019, the county just outside of our nation's capital that I live in and by the next year, was being expanded into a year-round social justice and anti-racist program for all grades. [6] Complete with BLM t-shirts and raised fists, this BLM curriculum is not anything like the Black History Month teaching of the past. It is a purely radical agenda that includes the following, and I am sure many of you will be shocked that this is really happening in our schools today.

1. **Restorative Justice:** We are committed to collectively, lovingly, and courageously working vigorously for freedom and justice for Black people and, by extension, all people. As we forge our path, we intentionally build and nurture a beloved community that is bonded together through a beautiful struggle that is restorative, not depleting.

2. **Empathy:** We are committed to practicing empathy; we engage comrades with the intent to learn about and connect with their contexts.

3. **Loving Engagement:** We are committed to embodying and practice justice, liberation, and peace in our engagements with one another.

---

5.   "Black Lives Matter 13 Guiding Principles." D.C. Area Educators for Social Justice. Accessed July 18, 2020. https://www.dcareaeducators4socialjustice.org/black-lives-matter/13-guiding-principles.

6.   Ryan, Kate. "'A new day': Prince George's County education leader on reopening schools." WTOP. Last modified July 6, 2020. https://wtop.com/coronavirus/2020/07/a-new-day-prince-georges-county-education-leader-on-reopening-schools/.

4. **Diversity:** We are committed to acknowledging, respecting, and celebrating difference(s) and commonalities.

5. **Globalism:** We see ourselves as part of the Global Black family and we are aware of the different ways we are impacted or privileged as Black folk who exist in different parts of the world.

6. **Queer Affirming:** We are committed to fostering a queer-affirming network. When we gather, we do so with the intention of freeing ourselves from the tight grip of heteronormative thinking or, rather, the belief that all in the world are heterosexual unless s/he or they disclose otherwise.

7. **Trans Affirming:** We are committed to embracing and making space for trans brothers and sisters to participate and lead. We are committed to being self-reflexive and doing the work required to dismantle cis-gender privilege and uplift Black trans folk, especially Black trans women who continue to be disproportionately impacted by trans-antagonistic violence.

8. **Collective Value:** We are guided by the fact all Black lives regardless of actual or perceived sexual identity, gender identity, gender expression, economic status, ability, disability, religious beliefs or disbeliefs, immigration status or location matter.

9. **Intergenerational:** We are committed to fostering an intergenerational and communal network free from ageism. We believe that all people, regardless of age, show up with capacity to lead and learn.

10. **Black Families:** We are committed to making our spaces family-friendly and enable parents to fully participate

with their children. We are committed to dismantling the patriarchal practice that requires mothers to work "double shifts" that require them to mother in private even as they participate in justice work.

11. **Black Villages:** We are committed to disrupting the Western-prescribed nuclear family structure requirement by supporting each other as extended families and "villages" that collectively care for one another, and especially "our" children to the degree that mothers, parents, and children are comfortable.

12. **Unapologetically Black:** We are unapologetically Black in our positioning. In affirming that Black Lives Matter, we need not qualify our position. To love and desire freedom for ourselves is a necessary prerequisite for wanting the same for others.

13. **Black Women:** We are committed to building a Black women affirming space free from sexism, misogyny, and male-centeredness.

Although there are admirable goals in this program like love, empathy, inclusion, extended families, and pride, these are mixed in with some very concerning "Guiding Principles," which is the political agenda that is the actual aim for Black Lives Matter programs. You will notice that white people are not a part of this program, nor are mixed-race families, nor the values of Christianity, nor the values of capitalism, nor any of the actual ideas of the Founding Fathers. You will notice they want to dismantle the nuclear family and that they call each other "comrades." It is a program dedicated to instilling Marxism in the minds of our children. Period.

If you never thought of homeschooling or private schooling as being necessary in our society, think again. And think again about all those times you didn't bother to vote for your local school board. What our children and grandchildren learn today may fundamentally change our society forever.

DAVE

What exactly are you getting when paying tens of thousands of dollars for a college education? It used to be thought of as a stepping-stone to a good job and a stable future. It still is if you pick a STEM degree, but for everyone else, your next stop might be employment at Starbucks. This isn't a new development; a bachelor's in liberal arts has been used as a punchline in jokes for decades. But now what we are seeing is a poisoning of the college system for all disciplines. I think back to when I attended college at the University of Hawaii in the early 2000s. Certainly a very liberal school, yet for the most part, the curriculum reflected the name of the course. Race, gender, and sexual orientation were not topics in Music 101 or Economics 300 courses. Instead, what I found were classes overly focused on overpriced, dry textbooks that were boring and unreadable. Standard fare for the education system in the United States.

I do, however, remember a course I took in community college in 1999, Philosophy 101. I expected that we would read Plato, Socrates, and some of the other well-known philosophers, and we did, but a third of our semester was dedicated to an entirely different topic. The professor, a woman in her sixties with short crew cut hair, had written her own book. Not on philosophy, but on the origin and history of female goddesses, which, according to her literature, predated male gods—a very important point that was repeated ad nauseum. I remember sitting in class staring at her eighty-page pamphlet completely bewildered. Was this even considered philosophy and why the hell is it Philosophy 101? Clearly, she had a viewpoint and an agenda that she wanted to push on her students. It was actually an interesting book, but I didn't feel it was appropriate for the class. At least, however, it was in the ballpark of what we were studying even if it took a sharp left turn.

But while a liberal teacher may insert her own agenda into the classroom, today's college administrators are taking this to a whole new level. First of all, if you are entering college, you may be required to take a racial sensitivity course as a freshman! After all, if you are a homeschooler or received a private school education, you might have missed out on being properly socialized and sensitized to the values of the Left. Are you a professor teaching accounting or physics? What do you think the opening question on your job interview will be? An inquiry into your proficiency of the subject? Are you good at communicating complex ideas? No, what the administrators want to know is how do you plan to inject issues of diversity into your classes? How do you plan on making people of color comfortable in a learning environment dominated by white faces? Yes, in 2020, these are the issues that preoccupy our college educators.

CHAPTER EIGHT

THE NEW MARXISM

IDENTITY POLITICS, SAFE SPACES, AND CULTURAL APPROPRIATION

"I have a dream that one day on the red hills of Georgia, the sons of former slaves and the sons of former slave owners will be able to sit together at the table of brotherhood."

MARTIN LUTHER KING, JR.[1]

PAT

My White Women Yoga Meetup investigation got the most outrage from white yoga teachers. Yes, white yoga teachers were incredibly incensed that I would have a group that locked out POC, specifically people from India as that is where yoga comes from. They were angry I was culturally appropriating a practice that wasn't mine to steal and certainly wasn't mine to steal and alter to my liking.

---

1.   Mindock, Clark. "Martin Luther King Jr: 50 quotes from the civil rights leader who inspired a nation." *Independent.* Last modified January 20, 2020. https://www.independent.co.uk/news/world/americas/martin-luther-king-quotes-death-assassination-mlk-jr-a8855071.html.

Hi Pat,

I'm just wondering why you need a yoga space exclusively for white women? Have you had some experience that's made yoga feel somehow unsafe? It's an ancient practice that originated in India - not a white community, so it's just very confusing that you're now creating a white's only space.

Lauren

I doubt Lauren is practicing in a majority Indian yoga group and doing anything more Hindu than clasping her palms together and saying, "Namaste." Oh, wait. Yoga originated in India as a highly religious ritual of the male priest caste, a spiritual practice related to ancient Hinduism,[2] hardly an exercise pastime for upper-middle-class white women wearing the latest yoga outfits and focusing on the awesomeness of their bodies. Meditation or the singing of bhajans is hardly even the smallest part of a normal US yoga class, but, then, I shouldn't nitpick. We can also ignore that the yoga brought to the US by early Indian yogi masters was transmogrified into a transcendental meditation craze and then into fitness fad (with a little mind/body consciousness thrown in) because it made yogis, teachers, and cult leaders a lot more money, fame, and followers than teaching disciples under a tree.[3] But, there I go, being nitpicky again. I shouldn't accuse you of cultural appropriation even though it seems to me you have never been to India or spent time with Indians or know squat about Hinduism.

---

2. "MASCULINITY AND YOGA: THE REVEALING HISTORY OF YOGA." The Treehouse Recovery PDX. Accessed July 18, 2020. https://treehouserecoverypdx.com/addiction-blog/masculinity-and-yoga-the-revealing-history-of-yoga/.

3. Hammond, Holly. "The Timeline and History of Yoga in America." *Yoga Journal*. Last modified December 12, 2018. https://www.yogajournal.com/yoga-101/yogas-trip-america.

But because I am not an SJW, it appears anything I do is cultural appropriation. Why? Because my sole purpose isn't to glorify another race or culture or to confess that they are better and admit (joyfully) that we white people didn't come up with that idea and that they, not I, will never be able to come close to executing whatever cultural achievement they have presented to the world. Why, if I attempt to cook or dance or dress or copy or fuse anything from another culture, it is theft and cruel and insulting (especially if I do it better). Why did SJWs work overtime to shut down two white ladies' burrito pop-up restaurant in Portland, Oregon? Because they were competition to Mexicans who owned burrito trucks or because they might make better burritos than someone from Mexican heritage? I didn't see any Mexicans complaining. They probably thought it was pretty neat that some American-born ladies loved Mexican food and wanted to make it themselves.

Matthew Korfage of the *Willamette Week* wrote in his column:

> But we really didn't anticipate that a short and positive review of a weekends-only breakfast burrito pop-up a couple of weeks ago would ignite an international incident—a rage-filled conversation about cultural appropriation that led to opinion pieces in the London Daily Mail and The Washington Post and on Fox News, not to mention on Mexican social media. It was a perfect storm.
>
> The photograph that ran with our May 17 review of Kooks depicted two young, middle-class-looking women triumphantly holding burritos up in the air. Our article described how the two women "lost their

minds" over handmade flour tortillas on an impromptu getaway to Puerto Nuevo, Mexico.

"I picked the brains of every tortilla lady there in the worst broken Spanish ever, and they showed me a little of what they did," Kooks co-owner Liz Connelly told WW.

"They told us the basic ingredients, and we saw them moving and stretching the dough similar to how pizza makers do before rolling it out with rolling pins. They wouldn't tell us too much about technique, but we were peeking into the windows of every kitchen, totally fascinated by how easy they made it look. We learned quickly it isn't quite that easy."

We've told similar stories about food inspiration many times in the past—two Portlanders who'd taken a motorcycle surfing trip to Mexico, fallen in love with grilled chicken and brought the recipe back home to their food cart; or Andy Ricker's trips to Thailand, on breaks from being a house painter, which led to Pok Pok and his celebrity status across the United States and in Thailand.

But this time, the story about Kooks provided tinder for a cultural inferno.

More than 1,500 comments were posted, with still thousands more on Facebook—some defending, others attacking the Kooks owners, who were derided as white "Beckys" even though one of the two Kooks owners is a quarter Chinese.

"This article is a clear example of how media perpetuates and reinforces racism and white supremacy, brandishing it as 'fun' and 'innovative,'" read one comment. Another demanded that the two women send remunerations back to Mexico for the cultural theft of tortilla recipes.[4]

Before cultural appropriation colored everything, cultural appreciation was a sign of forward thinking, of a *lack* of racist tendencies, and a willingness to share the joys of cultures one is not necessarily a part of. People of those cultures used to take it as a compliment that their art or music or food or other cultural specialties were being recognized, not as necessarily better, but recognized as a wonderful contribution to the world. What's not to like about Indian food, Mexican fiestas, reggae music, Jewish bagels, Neapolitan Pizza, and Nigerian fufu (okay, my kids hate fufu, which is ground yams that go great with groundnut stew, but I love that stuff). And what's not to like about Hawaiian singer Israel Kamakawiwo'ole's wonderful rendition of "Over the Rainbow"? A Polynesian guy redid a song composed by American Jews and sung by Judy Garland, and I don't hear anyone complaining.

I have been to India five times. I have always worn a sari or a salwar kameez outfit, and never have I had a negative response from an Indian. For that matter, I got many nice comments about wearing the national dress and how I looked so nice. Likewise, when I ate with my hand, I got a nice compliment about how I am so Indian! Indians and Indian Americans have always seemed to appreciate my love of their culture, and never once was I accused of appropriating it. When I perform Bollywood dances in front of an Indian

---

4.   Korfhage, Matthew. "The Battle Over Kooks Burritos Led to Death Threats and International Outrage. We Invited Portland Chefs to Weigh in." *Willamette Week*. Last modified September 11, 2017. https://www.wweek.com/restaurants/news-restaurants/2017/06/06/the-battle-over-kooks-burritos-led-to-death-threats-and-international-outrage-we-invited-portland-chefs-to-weigh-in/.

audience, many come up to me afterward and tell me how much they enjoyed my dancing.

"Auntie, you dance so nicely! Just like an Indian!"

This is the kind of world I want to live in: one that can share cultures and not be angry about the fusing or imitating of ideas and the sheer love of others' ideas! I don't mind a bit if Hindus put up a Christmas tree or want to borrow my recipe for Jewish donuts and my German family's cookie recipes. I love when people from other cultures want to experience the culture of the US or Maryland or even, gasp, white people's culture!

In 2013, I published a novel called *Only the Truth*. Although my publisher at Hyperion loved it and said it reminded her of books by John Steinbeck (oh, what a compliment even if I am nowhere close), she said she could not publish it because she didn't know how to market it as I am a white author and the main character and a number of other main characters are black. Yes, because I was not an African American author, she didn't know where the book would fit in at the bookstore or how to advertise it! It was a psychological literary murder mystery, and though it has an old-fashioned feel, I didn't see why it couldn't be in either the mystery or literary section. My guess is that she was worried the book would be attacked as cultural appropriation.

How is that? The main character was a composite of my Jamaican ex-husband and an African American renter in my home. Of course, the actual character in my book took on a personality of his own, and Sweet Billy Ray was not one nor the other. Another character was based on my mother-in-law, but that character developed into her own self. The police chief in the book was based in my head on Dwayne Johnson, also known as The Rock. Why? I think just because he made a good fantasy for me! Sadly, he told me that he wouldn't accept the role in the movie because his character didn't have enough of an action role. Ah, well. A girl can dream!

I ended up self-publishing the book because my agent couldn't find a publisher willing to go with a white author writing a book with major black characters. I got lucky in that the book did very well in sales on Amazon and was well-loved by the readers. Still, it was frustrating that the book wasn't able to be on the shelves in bookstores because of the racial "issues." Oddly, the book had nothing to do with racial issues; it was just the perception of cultural appropriation that prevented it from getting a traditional publisher.

And there is proof this is a huge issue now for authors. Oprah lauded the book *American Dirt* by Jeanine Cummins as a very sensitive and timely novel of the American-Mexican border issues and the desperate plight of illegal immigrants trying to make it into the US so that they might be spared the dangers and difficulties of the life they were fleeing in Mexico or Guatemala or Nicaragua.

One would think liberals would be in love with this book! The reviews came out, and almost every reviewer raved about the book, and the sales soared. Then, some leftists got hold of the idea that the author wasn't brown enough. Sure, she had a Puerto Rican grandmother, but that wasn't good enough. It wasn't enough that she did all that research in Mexico and in migrant shelters and in the soup kitchen she worked in across the border in Tijuana, and it wasn't enough that she did all those interviews with humanitarian aid workers.[5] I guess that means the fine novels written by John Steinbeck, Ernest Hemingway,

---

5. Charles, Ron. "Threats against the author of 'American Dirt' threaten us all." *The Washington Post.* Accessed July 18, 2020. https://www.washingtonpost.com/entertainment/books/death-threats-against-the-author-of-american-dirt-threaten-us-all/2020/01/30/ec5070e8-430d-11ea-aa6a-083d01b3ed18_story.html.

and James Michener had no business being published because they were also writing about cultures that were not their own.

I read *American Dirt*, and I liked it. It felt like Mexico and Central America to me (and I have been all over Mexico and Nicaragua and Guatemala). I sympathized with the characters fleeing from the drug cartels and MS-13 and from poverty and hopelessness. Even though I disagree with open-border policies and with the idea of paying coyotes to smuggle illegals into the country, it doesn't mean I cannot empathize with these suffering people and think the book is worth reading and discussing.

So, oddly, a conservative likes the book and the Left, who the book should speak to, wants the book banished. That is the nonsense of cultural appropriation today. It is pure identity politics and separatism.

DAVID

As a kid growing up in the '90s, there were no safe spaces or even the idea that persons of color needed a corner for themselves to be free from persecution. Ironically, it was as an adult in an era where we had our first black president that I finally realized that I did, indeed, need a safe space. I had been the victim of insults and condescension, treated like a pariah, and had my skin color referenced in conversation. Had I accidentally wandered into a Klan rally? No, the Klan doesn't have much of a presence here in Maryland. Maybe I had inadvertently bumped into an informal meeting of white nationalists during happy hour at the pub? Nope. These comments weren't from fire-breathing, knuckle-dragging Trump supporters, but from tolerant and accepting liberals. If they were white liberals, the comment is, "How can you be a conservative if you're black?" It's curious to note the level of their anger and frustration, as if I owed it to them to be a Democrat, as if to say, "Have you no appreciation for the fact that I defend black people and support civil rights?" Just like the plantation owner who says to his slaves, "Don't I treat you better than the other owners?" It's a very condescending and paternalistic attitude they display, and it is completely lost on them.

I remember a specific incident back in 2008. I was living abroad in Chennai, India, where I was studying economics. My lodgings were a YMCA that served as sort of a hotel/long-term living quarters for foreigners traveling abroad. One morning, I met two brothers who were college professors in their late sixties who were staying briefly at the YMCA before traveling to other destinations in south India. The YMCA served breakfast in the mess hall, and they invited me to join them. This was the summer when the campaigns of Barack Obama and John McCain were in full swing, where it was becoming apparent that Obama was the favorite. In hindsight, it really was a unique period in our history, and the energy and enthusiasm of Americans, especially black Americans, was at a high. These two gentlemen sitting across from a young black American in his twenties couldn't wait to ask me how I felt. I can still see them sitting there, brimming with excitement and eagerly anticipating my thoughts. Boy, were they disappointed! I don't think I could have gotten a more disgruntled response if I had stood up and pissed in their breakfast masala dosa. I almost felt bad for ruining the morning...almost.

So, let's be clear. Being a black conservative is not easy. I find it a bit ironic that fellow persons of color accuse you of being an Uncle Tom, the implication being that you are looking for an easy out. Perhaps they are unaware, but my life would be *much* easier if I were a liberal Democrat. Being a black Republican is the road less traveled, with much more grief. But, no, I don't need a safe space. Conflict makes you grow and adapt. You won't find very many dumb black conservatives. With the positions we hold, we will be challenged, ostracized, and forced to truly understand the philosophy that girds our thinking. This is a lesson that Democrat Representative Ted Lieu found out the hard way when he attempted to character assassinate a black conservative woman by the name of Candace Owens during congressional hearings. The hearing was on the issue of white nationalism, and Owens had been invited to testify by the GOP. During the hearing, Congressman Lieu played a clip of Owens talking about Hitler, but devoid of context. He hoped to embarrass and shame her, but instead was made to look the fool by Owen's concise and scathing rebuttal.[6] He should have known better; with a black female in front of him, he was robbed of every leftist's favorite tools when in an argument: accusations of racism and sexism. That's what makes us so dangerous! We force liberals to defend their ideas on their own merits, and for them, that's a losing proposition.

The attitude and treatment of black conservatives from a political party and ideology that claim to have a monopoly on racial enlightenment and equality can be mind-bogglingly insulting, if not overtly racist. One of my favorite political cartoons is one of an angry and belligerent donkey holding a shotgun in search of his runaway slave. That's how it sometimes feels to be a black conservative. You're looked at like a traitor from your own brethren and as an ungrateful by white liberals.

---

6.   Martosko, David. "Candace Owens Becomes Breakout Black Conservative Star for Slamming Rep. Ted Lieu." *Daily Mail Online*. Last modified April 10, 2019. https://www.dailymail.co.uk/news/article-6905383/Candace-Owens-breakout-black-conservative-star-slamming-Rep-Ted-Lieu.html.

They may not say this openly, but every once in a while, they will let it slip. My new favorite candid moment is when Democrat candidate Joe Biden in his interview with Charlamagne tha God made a rather unfortunate mistake. In a moment where his filter failed to work, although in the case of Biden I'm not sure if he ever had one, he said this: "If you have a problem figuring out whether you are for me or Trump, then you ain't black."[7] Imagine that, a seventy-eight-year-old white politician who has spent over fifty years in Washington telling black people what makes them black. It's so preposterous that you kinda have to laugh, although it would be less concerning if he'd said that from his retirement villa in Boca Raton and not as a candidate for president of the United States. Ridiculous, but his statement reflects the sentiment of many across the Democrat Party and progressive ideology. The true believers fundamentally do not understand how a black person could be conservative and Republican, and trying to explain it to them is a fruitless endeavor.

Condescension is the other tactic used to belittle minorities who stray off the plantation. Growing up, one of the most inspiring books I read was *Gifted Hands* by Ben Carson. For decades, it was widely accepted that he was the leading pediatric neurosurgeon in the world. Certainly, he is no idiot. But then he made the grievous error of running for president as a Republican, two decades of universal praise vanished into thin air. They even printed a few articles critical of his record as a neurosurgeon which, of course, is laughable. In a more subtle display of contempt, they dropped the Dr. from his title. Dr.

---

7.   Sotomayor, Marianna, and Mike Memoli. "Biden Apologizes for Saying African Americans 'Ain't Black' If They Back Trump Re-Election." NBCUniversal News Group. Last modified May 22, 2020. https://www.nbcnews.com/politics/2020-election/biden-tells-african-americans-you-ain-t-black-if-they-n1212911.

Ben Carson became Ben Carson. Meanwhile, no anchor on CNN or MSNBC would dare utter the name Christine Blasey-Ford without including her academic title of doctor. Equality and black representation in government is a rallying cry for the Left, but only for those blacks who stay loyal to the party. Put an R next to your name, and all bets are off.

PAT

There is one group, oddly the largest group racially in the United States, that no longer is allowed to be proud of its roots and culture. White people can no longer feel any kind of specialness. For that matter, they can only despise themselves. This is what the protests of 2020 made a point of. I remember seeing one of the saddest photos ever on Twitter: a mother who had made her six-year-old daughter hold a placard that had the words "White Privilege" in the middle with an arrow pointed up at her white child's face. Underneath was written #BlackLivesMatter. Already this liberal mother was brainwashed into shaming her daughter, having her daughter apologize for being born white even though, at six years old, she hardly has had time to mistreat blacks or any other persons of color. In fact, she might not even know that skin color has any meaning at all.

But, to be sure, this child will grow up mentally flagellating herself all through her life. She will learn from Black Lives Matter in her school that her ancestors were all evildoers who ruined the next hundreds of years for descendants of slaves. She will learn that Latinos were put in cages and forced to learn a language that they were uncomfortable with and that the refusal of the United States to become bilingual has kept them down. She will learn that doing yoga or wearing a kimono or sari is cultural appropriation from Asians. She will learn that whites can never be anything but racists, Nazis, and white supremacists.

And as a group, whites should never, ever put themselves in positions to make people of color subservient. I guess that means no whites should be voted into office, no whites should be teachers, no whites should be police officers, no whites should be bosses because whites simply cannot exist without having implicit bias, without being unconsciously racist if not overtly racist. They cannot be trusted and they cannot ever understand people of color well enough to be able to treat them appropriately. Whites should simply not exist.

Isn't that sweet? This is the message that the protests of 2020 were really about. There were actually huge groups of whites prostrating themselves in front of black people who were telling them to repeat phrases in unison like "I have white privilege" and "I will love my black neighbors the same as my white neighbors." Can you imagine black people bowing down before white people and repeating such phrases? There would be a massive outcry about the humiliation and degradation of such an act.

This is how apartheid begins. And if this bizarre way of thinking becomes an even worse virus than COVID-19, our country will self-destruct in the not too distant future.

CHAPTER NINE

OUR PROGRESSIVE LEADERS
A RACE LEFT TOWARD MADNESS

> "I am not interested in power for power's sake, but I'm interested in power that is moral, that is right and that is good."
>
> MARTIN LUTHER KING, JR.[1]

PAT

I pulled up to the Canadian border with my three small children in the back (two brown, one black). The border guard looked at me, looked in the back at my kids, and asked, "Are those your children?"

I looked at him with horror and then whipped my head around to see them. "Oh, my God! I always thought they were!" I looked back at the guard with a distressed look on my face. He cracked up.

"Go on!" He handed my passport back and waved my car through with a grin.

---

1.   Mindock, Clark. "Martin Luther King Jr: 50 quotes from the civil rights leader who inspired a nation." *Independent.* Last modified January 20, 2020. https://www.independent.co.uk/news/world/americas/martin-luther-king-quotes-death-assassination-mlk-jr-a8855071.html.

Sometimes people aren't being racist; they are just doing their job, and one would think the point of a guard on the border is that he is to guard the border. I remember on our honeymoon, my husband and I had to cross the border from Guatemala into Belize. We boarded the bus, and also on the bus was a hippie couple. We heard that Belize was very tough about people coming into their country with little money and then becoming a nuisance. Yes, they were worried about white people abusing their welcome.

Quite frankly, my husband and I were pretty low on money as well, and we were planning to stay in a super cheap place and eat street food until we flew home a week later. But Belize had a minimum requirement for entering the country; you had to have a reasonable sum of money to be a proper tourist. I told my husband I was going to change my clothes in the back of the bus. I threw a pretty dress over my shorts and T-shirt and put a pair of heels on. Then we followed the hippies off of the bus.

As we stood in the line, we heard the hippies arguing with the border guard and then turn back, upset that they had been refused entry. When my husband and I got to the border guards and they saw we had not so much money ourselves, I told them that my daddy was wiring me money to a bank in Belize City and that we were on our honeymoon. The guard noted my style of dress and allowed us into the country, confident I was telling the truth. Funny, every country I have traveled to has strict immigration policies. Some are extremely difficult for Americans to get a visa for, even for countries Americans are unlikely to have any interest in moving to permanently.

But America? Why should we have borders at all? Let's just let the entire population of Central and South America come on in! No money? No problem! No English? No problem! No skills? No problem! It's a one-way street, and we need to put up some serious roadblocks. It has nothing to do with racism or not liking people from other cultures. It is not about being heartless toward desperate people who want to escape violence and poverty. It is about our country being able to survive into the future, and no country can survive without a reasonable, sustainable immigration policy that is based on what benefits the country.

DAVE

Open borders are part of an overall strategy by progressives to form a permanent majority in the United States. Double the number of immigrants who identify as Democrats rather than Republicans.[2] With that clear majority, it is only a matter of time before the demographics give progressives an ironclad grip on national politics, a one-party system with progressives in complete control of all three branches of government. Were this to happen, the Republican Party would become an irrelevant minority whose only power would exist at the state level. We are very close to reaching this tipping point, a point of no return, hence the rabid attacks on Donald Trump and his attempts to bring law and order to our southern border. Despite the fact that Republicans stand to lose their grip on national politics, a surprising number of Republicans have been quiet or, even worse, have impeded President Trump's efforts. This can be exemplified by the number of Republicans who supported

---

2.   York, Byron. "Study finds more immigrants equals more Democrats --- and more losses for GOP ." *Washington Examiner*. Last modified April 15, 2014. https://www.washingtonexaminer.com/study-finds-more-immigrants-equals-more-democrats-and-more-losses-for-gop.

Hillary Clinton, some of whom were actually past Republican presidents. When it comes to the issue of immigration, the Establishment Republican position is pro-illegal immigration irrespective of the wishes of the base. This is, in part, the reason that Donald Trump outlasted his mainstream Republican competitors; on the issue of immigration, he distinguished himself, and the voter felt he wasn't all talk but actually meant to do something about it.

And there is a reason why the issue of immigration is so volatile with Republican voters: countless times previous Republican presidents and Republican-controlled Congresses promised to fix the issue, only to do nothing. In 1986, under President Reagan, amnesty was given with the promise that improved border security would follow; however, since that amnesty, which legalized 3.6 million illegal aliens, the number of those living illegally in the country has risen dramatically. As of 2019, it is estimated that there are between ten and twelve million illegal immigrants living in the USA, making up over 3 percent of the population.[3] Did either terms of President Bush bring us closer to a solution? Nope. Enter 2016 with the "front-runner" Jeb Bush. To quote his brother George, "Fool me once, shame on you. Fool me twice, shame on...shame...well, the point is you can't be fooled twice."[4] We weren't. Jeb was quickly jettisoned, along with the other Establishment Republicans. Conservatives had finally had enough, and time is short. Break glass in a case of an emergency. We did, and out walked Trump.

---

3.   Kamarck, Elaine, and Christine Stenglein. "How many undocumented immigrants are in the United States and who are they?" *Brookings*. Last modified November 12, 2019. https://www.brookings.edu/policy2020/votervital/how-many-undocumented-immigrants-are-in-the-united-states-and-who-are-they/.

4.   "Top 10 Bushisms." *Time*. Last modified January 11, 2009. http://content.time.com/time/specials/packages/article/0,28804,1870938_1870943_1870944,00.html.

PAT

And did *that* send the Left into a frenzy. Truly, they lost their minds! First, they claimed that Hillary really won the election by the popular vote even though that is not the way our system works. Then, they went after President Trump by trying to destroy his reputation with the Steele Dossier, replete with one of the ickiest sexual aberrations—golden showers—during a fabricated romp with prostitutes in a hotel in Russia. Then his choices for the Supreme Court were disparaged, not just for their record as judges but for their characters, and they hosted a most unbelievably humiliating bogus trial—yes, it was surely a trial—of Judge Brett Kavanaugh. When they lost that round because they could not come up with proof or even a believable story from their star witness, Christine Blasey Ford, and when the other phony accusers brought forth by the now incarcerated Michael Avenatti who worked overtime with CNN to destroy Donald Trump via adult porn star Stormy Daniels also blew up, they moved on to another strategy. It was time to try to impeach the president. First, there was the whole Russian collusion hoax and the Mueller investigation, which failed to come up with anything damning after wasting a huge amount of time and taxpayer money. When that failed, the Democrat Congress moved on to the Ukraine hoax, which was based on the slimmest of "evidence," the wording of one sentence during a phone call President Trump made to the President Zelensky. If I tried to write a fiction book with such a bizarre set of intrigues, any publisher I would have sent the manuscript in to would have laughed at me and told me the scenarios were totally implausible. When they say, "Truth is stranger than fiction," they ain't kidding.

If all of these completely outrageous political attacks from the Left were not enough to destroy our president and our political system, the regular folks of the Left, the voting Democrats, growing increasingly frustrated that conservatives had actually succeeded in getting their candidate into the White House, began exhibiting increasingly bizarre behavior. From marching on Washington with pussy hats on their heads, to protesting the new president simply because he wasn't their choice (Hillary was), to the overreaction toward a pitiful band of supposed white supremacists and one crazy loon in Charlottesville, to the rise of Antifa, to wimpy soy boys in stupid masks attacking conservatives on the streets, to the vicious media attacks on the conservative schoolboys of Covington participating in the March for Life rally in Washington. Oh, lord, what an exhausting few years since the inauguration of President Trump in 2017. Add to this the increase in separatism for blacks and people of color—safe spaces, separate dorm floors where whites are not allowed to reside, graduation ceremonies for nonwhites only, a refusal of universities to allow conservative speakers—it seemed the fabric of society was not only fraying, it was being ripped apart by pit bulls of the Left.

But this was only the beginning of the insanity. The depth of loss of rational thinking by the Left didn't make itself known until the Ukraine hoax failed to unseat President Trump. It appeared, with the economy roaring to the best economy in decades (and with even minority communities seeing great economic gains), there was no way he was not going to win a second term—a concept that was poison to the Democrats and the Left.

Then came the coronavirus. Oh, how unbelievably fortunate for these desperate liberals that they had one more chance to take down the president. Once the original two-week plan was carried out for all citizens of the country, barring essential workers, to quarantine themselves at home and the media could run with the most fearmongering tales of massive death rates if the citizens dared to come out of their caves, the closing of America for months became their way to destroy the economy, to destroy private business, to destroy the entire future of the country.

What kind of people are these leftist leaders who would rather send millions of people into starvation (oh, excuse me, "food insecurity"), into homelessness, into a massive depression, into insolvency, and into massive inflation to the point where their savings would be worthless, rather than accept a conservative president for the next four years and be happy to have a continuing excellent economy that makes America great for all? Evil people, evil people, that is all I can say. Evil that comes from a narcissistic, distorted view of one's self and one's importance, evil that arises from selfishness, and dare I say it, from a Marxist mentality.

But even *that* wasn't enough! One incident of assumed police misconduct in Minneapolis, and there wasn't just an in-depth discussion or more kneeling or controlled protests; there was rioting and looting and burning and demands for America to admit to institutionalized racism and for the entire system to be…what? Changed? No one actually said how it should be changed (except for unseating President Trump). Because if one says the problem of racism is in our DNA, then it is hopeless to expect those people (those white people) to change significantly enough to make things better. If one says that history proves racism is imbedded in our institutions and we must vote to change them, why haven't those Democrats who have been running a good portion of those institutions had any success? Well, then I guess the only thing left is revolution and a whole new political system. That is exactly the one and only solution they are demanding.

DAVE

World War II is probably the last time our country was completely united in a single goal: the desire to defeat Adolf Hitler and the Axis powers. The war in Korea stalemated, Vietnam turned into a disaster, and the first Gulf War only escaped deep scrutiny due to its brevity. Post 9/11, there were a few months where it seemed we had national unity in hunting down the Taliban in Afghanistan. Eventually, though, the mood soured and war in the Middle East became the controversy that to this day we are still debating. Little did we know, the next great threat would not be another war half around the world, but COVID-19, which is largely believed to have originated in Wuhan, China. Since Trump took office in 2017, our relationship with China has been tumultuous, and it should be as we are barely scratching the surface when we shine a light on their malicious activities toward the United States. Currency manipulation, intellectual property theft, and as we are finding out, moles within our educational institutions that steal research data and send it back to the "motherland." We are only seeing the tip of the iceberg with regards to the Chinese Communist government's operations against the United States.

Unintentionally, or perhaps intentionally, their greatest blow to the US was the novel coronavirus that first appeared in Wuhan. At the time this book is being written, we still don't know if it actually originated from an outdoor wet market or from a Wuhan lab only meters down the street. The Chinese, of course, vehemently deny it escaped from one of their labs. Of course, any rational person would look at their track record of lies and deceit and immediately question the veracity of their statements. They did lie about the virus and how it transmitted, they did lie about its containment, and they did use the WHO to perpetuate their falsehoods, which we know now led to a delayed response from US and other western countries.

They told their citizens across the world to gather up medicals supplies like masks and send them back to China in order to bolster their supplies before the rest of the world caught wind. They threatened the US with cutting off of vital pharmaceutical supply chains. China, through their deception, may be responsible for more dead Americans than all the wars going back to Korea put together.[5,6] One would think, now more than ever, Americans—Democrat and Republican, liberal and conservative—would come together to condemn the communist government in China for the global pandemic that has crushed the entire planet. Wrong.

I can only imagine what it would have been like for Franklin D. Roosevelt in 1941 when the US declared war on Germany if a sizable chunk of the mainstream press were parroting Nazi propaganda. Unfortunately, in the midst of a crisis spawned from our greatest geopolitical adversary of the twenty-first century, our press is doing just that. An article on Yahoo! has

---

5. "America's War." Department Of Veteran Affairs, November 2019. https://www.va.gov/opa/publications/factsheets/fs_americas_wars.pdf.

6. "Coronavirus Disease 2019 (COVID-19)." Centers for Disease Control and Prevention. Accessed August, 2020. https://www.cdc.gov/coronavirus/2019-ncov/cases-updates/cases-in-us.html.

debunked the idea that the Chinese coronavirus escaped from a lab in China. How you might wonder? Because the lab director said so! Here an American journalist takes the word of an individual who would disappear, never to be seen again, if the statements he made went contrary to the official story given by the Chinese government. Perhaps this same journalist would have asked Goebbels for his opinion on the validity of the invasion of Normandy. In the US Senate, former presidential candidate Kamala Harris proposed a bill condemning phrases like "Chinese virus" and "Wuhan virus" and, more comically, "Kung Flu" as being anti-Asian. As morgues in New York City overflow, our great senator from California is not preoccupied by the deception of the Chinese government, but instead wants to virtue signal about racism against Asians. How do we fight an enemy when our progressive media and politicians refuse to acknowledge the enemy?

This my great fear moving forward. I understand we will always have political division; we are a free country, and the result of freedom is diversity of thought and opinion. But we have gone beyond that. If our progressive leaders have so far drifted away from traditional liberalism into woke politics, we will effectively be neutered in the next great fight to come. Make no mistake; it will come. It's inevitable. Whereas Nazi Germany was a straightforward and obvious threat, China is much more slippery. They understand the long game and have played it masterfully the last thirty years, and time is not on our side. Projections show that the Chinese economy will overtake the US economy in the near future. They are aggressively expanding in southeast Asia and making forays into Africa in an attempt to gobble up natural resources. The coronavirus could be the misstep that the world needs to bring China to heel, but it is not encouraging. President Trump has made a great effort to contain the ever expanding sphere of Chinese influence,[7] but if progressive leaders in Congress refuse to recognize China for the bad player it is and has been, they may be able to slip through. I can only imagine President Xi, marveling that, after bringing the entire planet to a halt, American politicians were busier attacking the American president than the Communist Party leader himself. Stalin would have been envious.

---

7. Wulfsohn, Joseph A. "Trump Announces Increased Tariffs on China in Latest Trade War Salvo." Fox News. Last modified August 23, 2019. https://www.foxnews.com/politics/trump-announces-raised-tariffs-on-china-to-take-effect-in-september-october.

CHAPTER TEN

WHO IS PUSHING BACK? WHERE ARE OUR CONSERVATIVE LEADERS?

"A genuine leader is not a searcher for consensus but a moulder of consensus."

-MARTIN LUTHER KING, JR.[1]

DAVE

Somewhere around the late '60s and early '70s, two labels became inflexible. Liberal—meaning open-minded and inclusive—and conservative—meaning close-minded and exclusive. For a few decades, young folks were expected to be liberal until they had a family and understood the struggle of keeping food on the table. Then they circled the wagons and became conservative; however, somewhere along the way, universities lost their classical instructors, and their replacements were young liberals who got tenure and never had to grow up. They became the Peter Pans of the campuses, and they represented

---

1. Mindock, Clark. "Martin Luther King Jr: 50 quotes from the civil rights leader who inspired a nation." *Independent.* Last modified January 20, 2020. https://www.independent.co.uk/news/world/americas/martin-luther-king-quotes-death-assassination-mlk-jr-a8855071.html.

a road to old age in which the naive, forever defiant mindset never settled down and became a citizen who wanted to ensure the stability of the country for the benefit of his children and their children.

The next generation of these liberal sorts grew up with parents who had lived through Woodstock and Vietnam and campus protests, as well as Black Power and riots and all things rebellious, and still wished for their leftist world as they reached their forties and fifties. Their children grew up believing all authority was oppressive and anyone not of a certain group is a victim. Their parents still pushed their liberal agendas in spite of the fact many of them had achieved the American Dream or at least had a good amount of opportunities to live a life that few in the world have the chance to even believe is possible. Somehow, these petulant parents managed to raise ungrateful children who think that unless they have a home with a chef's kitchen and a master bath with two sinks by the age of twenty-five, life has failed them. They think it is a sign they will never have the wealth of their parents (who lived in a fourth-floor walkup apartment at their age). They grumble and whine and believe they are the victims of a powerful elite, the white supremacists that run the country and will never give them (white or POC) a true chance.

And so, those old white men must go, and the old system of capitalism must go.

Yet the only thing many of these young people may truly have been a victim of is our leftist educational system, which has taught them to hate their own country.

PAT

When I volunteered at a school for the deaf in Punjab, India, a few years ago, I was impressed by the display of patriotism every morning by the schoolchildren. They would stand outside in rows in front of the Indian flag and raise their right arm in a salute and repeat the pledge. There were no dissidents as the students didn't expect their country to be perfect; they just expected that their country was *their* country and it was up to them to make it the best country possible. There was no little brat being told by his parent to take a knee because, in India, that child would be looking for a new school the following day. When one attended any ceremony, sports event, or even took a flight on an Indian plane, all speeches end with the saying "Jaí Hind!" which means "Hail India!" A spirit of patriotism is acceptable in that country and not considered a slap in the face to every group that feels they have not made it to the top level of society.

I am sure some liberals will claim this sounds an awful lot like Germany under Hitler, but just because one group of people misuses something (the Nazis rather stole the swastika from India and turned it 45 degrees, making it the emblem of the Nazi party instead of a symbol of divinity and spirituality), this doesn't mean that a concept is totally corrupt. Patriotism isn't about hating other countries; it's about appreciating where we live and wanting to make it a success (in a legal and ethical way). What was impressive in India was that children and adults, while recognizing the many problems their country was facing (poverty, pollution, corruption, and so on), still felt a love for and a responsibility to their country. It is true many leave India because opportunities elsewhere in the world are too alluring (the United States is the first choice), but that doesn't mean they feel a need to disparage the country they were born in and have grown up in. We Americans could learn to have this kind of loyalty as well—not blind loyalty, but a love for the land one is a part of, a love of family, and a love of community. We Americans should stand up for our country as well.

DAVE

In 1874, Thomas Nast, often considered the father of the modern-day political cartoon, chose an elephant to represent the, at that time, recently formed Republican Party. His choice of an elephant wasn't necessarily flattering. His cartoon depicted a scared, lumbering animal named the "Republican Vote" plodding toward a pit labeled "inflation" and "chaos." He would use the elephant again in future cartoons, and eventually the Republican Party would adopt it as its official symbol. Makes sense, an intelligent and wise creature, not a terrible choice for a political mascot; however, if Nast had a time machine, I doubt he would have picked an elephant, and that is not what comes to mind when looking at current Republican leadership. Perhaps a jellyfish would be more appropriate, or maybe some skittish marsupial. It seems that Republicans are either backpedaling from some comment they made that dared offend progressives, or when a contentious issue is in the national debate, they are MIA. Only the most egregious acts of slander by Democrats against Supreme Court nominee Brett Kavanaugh forced Republicans to grow a backbone. It was a welcome sight, if only enjoyed for a few weeks. That episode squarely in the rearview, they quickly returned to their spineless defaults.

The enemy only attacks people who are a real threat. Think which individuals get roundly bandied about in the media as objects of scorn. Before Trump, it was Rush Limbaugh, Sean

Hannity, Mark Levin, and a handful of others in conservative media, but very few actual members of Congress. This should be of great concern. When Senate Majority Leader Mitch McConnell incurs few attacks by the mainstream media, it correlates directly to the threat he imposes on the progressive agenda, which is very little. Say what you want about the Democrats in Congress, but they have no shortage of loudmouths and grandstanders pushing for their agenda and elbowing each other out for airtime. If the Republican Party stands a chance against the progressive onslaught, our leaders must reside in Congress, not in a studio in south Florida. Rush Limbaugh may inspire millions, but he casts zero votes on the floor of the Senate. Unfortunately, it seems that many congressional Republicans have been content to wait out Trump, hoping to keep themselves unscathed until he is far from office, ready to prostrate themselves in front of the media, saying, "Hey, I wasn't really a big supporter. Please let me stay in the club." If we conservatives truly want to follow through on the changes brought about through Trump, our next step is to find other Trumps at the local and state level and elect them into office.

While we do have a small group of conservative commentators with the best intentions, unfortunately not every voice is constructive. Donald Trump's inspiring campaign message that galvanized conservatives, bringing a hope of substantive change to Washington, DC, smacked hard into the realities of a deeply corrupt and powerful system. Even before he stepped foot into the Oval Office, members of the intelligence community, most notably the FBI and CIA, were plotting to destroy his administration. His national security advisor, Michael Flynn, walked into a trap sprung by some of the most corrupt officials in the FBI. Their plan? Get him fired or get him jailed.

Faceless bureaucrats whipped into high gear, leaking incomplete and damaging information to their favorite members of the press. By the time of his inauguration, the narrative was set. Donald Trump conspired with the Russian government to win the 2016 election. He was an illegitimate president who needed to be removed by any means necessary. A special counsel was assigned, and the AG of New York also began to investigate his businesses. His son, Don Jr., was dragged in front Congress under oath and grilled about a meeting in Trump Tower with a Russian lawyer. By the time the special counsel and his team had finished their investigation, no Russian collusion was found; however, his personal attorney had been jailed, his former campaign manager, Paul Manafort, was also thrown into prison, and his longtime associate, Roger Stone, was also looking at a lengthy prison sentence. There has never been a more brazen attempt to remove a sitting president. Yet some former supporters turned detractors don't think enough progress has been made. When 80 percent of his agenda had been enacted, they are mad that it was not 85 percent. And if it were 85 percent, they would argue it should be 90 percent. Are their intentions to further the MAGA agenda or self-promote? Ask yourself, does this person have any skin in the game? What have they sacrificed? Has their family been attacked? Have they been threatened with prosecution by crooked political government attorneys? Sadly, these voices are more consumed with Twitter followers and retweets than being a team player.

I, too, get frustrated, but I look at progress in context of the realities of our political system. One comment President Obama made that I do think is accurate is that political movement happens in small increments. You can go into the office of the presidency with the best intentions, but our system was designed to keep one man from having too much power, even if that man is president. Our judicial system gives judges immense power to halt executive actions taken by the president. Imagine that one judge, who is anonymous and unknown to 99.999 percent of the population, can temporarily halt an executive order by a man voted for by tens of millions of Americans. Like it or not, that is how our system is designed, and why the Left pulled out all the stops to prevent Brett Kavanaugh from being confirmed as a Supreme Court justice. And even if you get a favorable court ruling, getting legislation to support our agenda is next to impossible. If Democrats have a majority in just one chamber of Congress, forget about it. Even when Republicans hold both chambers, a combination of parliamentary rules and slippery two-faced Republicans again prevent the legislation we want from getting passed. There are lot of Republicans who, on TV, say all the right things but, in private to their allies and co-conspirators, express a loathing for Donald Trump. He has exposed their uselessness, corruption, and cowardice.

The MAGA agenda will make progress, but it will not move at the pace we all would like. Take a lesson from the Communists; they plan and scheme for decades to make the changes they want, yet they persist. It's actually the one quality about them I admire; they never give up and they keep coming, like waves hitting the beach. We, too, must find this tenacity. Don't be a fair-weather MAGA fan, dejected and deflated at the first sign of resistance. We have a great example of how to fight in President Trump. Never has a president been so abused in office, gone through so many horrific trials. But he has never collapsed. He has fought back and fought hard. Why? Because he loves his country. He listened to his constituents, more than any president in history. Follow his cue. Together, we can take back this country if we persevere, stay engaged, and resist the urge to fall into complacency. That is the main goal of our corrupt media: to demoralize you so you give up. Remember, they can't win unless you fold. Stay strong.

PAT

> "I always wanted to live in a third world country and now I don't have to move."
>
> —PAT BROWN

It is clear to me an awful lot of people on the Left haven't ever been to third-world or socialist countries, so they live in some odd fantasy world that these places are utopias with no racism and equality for all. Even for folks on the Right, they haven't spent enough or any time in a third-world or socialist country to engender enough fear of what kind of life these countries give to their citizens to inspire them to fight against the Left and their policies.

If these third-world locations are such wonderful places to live, why are huge numbers of people from many of these countries doing everything possible to come to America—even breaking the law to cross our borders, risking rape of mothers and daughters, and the deaths of their children along the way? Why are they so desperate for a better life and to have the ability to earn a decent living that they will leave their families behind to gamble on a positive outcome?

In spite of what should be a pretty obvious sign of how things are going in these folks' home countries, the Left thinks it would be a grand idea to import their style of governance to our country to fix all of our problems!

I ran a trip a couple of years ago to Cuba, a trip for older women. It was my most popular of the tours I ran in which women shared budget rooms, rode in chicken buses, and immersed themselves in the culture as much as I could offer. Cuba was the most requested of all the trips, not so much because it was off-limits to Americans for so long, but because this (mostly) very liberal group of ten ladies I took with me wanted to see the land of Castro and Che, their heroes from the time they were college students and thought of themselves as revolutionaries. Well, at least in spirit since they never really did anything all that revolutionary and grew up to be business-women and lived a rather suburban, upper middle-class life. But Cuba! Yes, the land that kept its values and camaraderie and didn't allow the US to change them into a capitalist country.

Did they notice when they flew over the country upon landing that the roads were almost devoid of vehicles? That there are almost no motorbikes, unlike countries like India where the roads are packed with them? Did they understand that those colorful old American cars that make every photo of Havana look charming is proof that few can afford a new car or even have an option to purchase one? How about those "buses" one sees in the town, a wagon with people on each side pulled by a horse? The selection of groceries is limited and often unavailable. To the visiting eye, all of this can seem quaint, old-fashioned, simple. But the reality is that the people are simply extraordinarily poor and the opportunities to improve one's life are scarce. The people are trapped under a tyrannical government and cannot escape (except by extraordinary methods) and, yet, this is a country some Americans seem to glorify.

I, too, enjoyed Cuba. I thought the people were very nice, the old crumbling architecture reminiscent of old Europe. The food didn't do much for me, but the mojitos made with Havana Club rum were awesome! The land itself, the mountains and the sea were beautiful. But I was not so blinded by leftist propaganda that I couldn't see Cuba drew the short stick when it came to rulers.

I love the cultures and the people of many countries. I even could live quite happily in a number of them (because I would be one of the rich people there). But I also realize that these places aren't perfect and the more these countries lean toward socialism, the less I have enjoyed being within their borders. Americans who are delusional about life under communism and socialism little realize the incredible luck we have that we live in a free country. We shouldn't piss it away.

DAVE

As conservatives we often point to the glaring failures of socialism and communism in the twentieth century as reason to reject those philosophies, and it is a pretty strong argument. Tens of millions dead, totalitarianism, and economic turmoil. Yet progressives are undeterred. Of course, the famous retort is the Trotsky argument that "it" just wasn't done right. With the proper people in place with the right conditions, paradise on earth could be upon us. Or some, like Bernie Sanders, will point to Nordic countries as examples of successful socialist countries already in existence. Do some of these countries have socialistic policies? Yes. Are they relatively wealthy Western countries? Sure. Can we copy them and achieve a similar result? Not a chance. Several factors that are often overlooked is the effect of culture, population, demographics, and geography on economic systems. In the case of Sweden or Norway, you have a relatively small, homogenous population with a culture where social cohesion innately exists. This doesn't imply that socialism works better there than capitalism; rather, socialism is far less damaging than it could be. As their population changes dues to immigration, their socialist paradise will encounter new problems that did not previously exist. Now, take socialism and implant it on a country of 300 million people, and you will create economic and financial upheaval that will be absolutely devastating.

Conservatives have to step up to the plate or will soon be counted as one of the third-world countries we've always worked hard to never become.

PAT

And we can't just depend on the vote to make our country great again. We, as individuals, must step up to the plate. It isn't easy, especially when stepping up to that plate can cost your friends, family members, your peace of mind, and your employment. I know because I have taken that route a number of times, and I can't say I came out of it personally better off. But I could sleep at night, and I could hope my stance made a difference in the long run.

We need people to take a stance in many venues. Our public education system is a disaster because it is pretty much run by the Democrat Party and our children are being trained to believe what they believe. What were just additions to Black History Month by the Black Lives Matter movement are now full-blown social justice programs added to the daily curriculum.[2] We have choices we can make to fight this. Along with voting for a better school board, parents can fight back, either within the system or by taking their children out of the system and sending them to private school or homeschooling. I chose to homeschool, and I've never regretted it.

Professors and teachers need to stand up for what is right. I developed the first Criminal Profiling Certificate Program in the country for Excelsior College. I worked very hard to make sure these five fifteen-week courses included exactly what knowledge and practical skills should be a good basis for any profiler or detective who wanted to do proper crime scene analysis. I got paid little for the courses, but I was promised (without a long-term contract) that I would be able to eventually develop a professor's guide for new instructors who came in after I got the program in motion and would eventually mentor and head the new profiling department.

As soon as I taught each course once and got the bugs out, lo and behold, new professors showed up to teach my finalized courses. They were not profilers but criminal justice teachers who had no clue how to analyze crime scenes. I saw them completely screw up teaching what happened at many crime scenes, and when I complained to the administration, I was ignored.

Worse, they had a system that is in place at many colleges and universities these days and is in use with adjunct professors. Students are permitted to evaluate their professors, and the administration will retain or let go of professors depending on their ratings. As I was a strict teacher, I wouldn't allow

2.   Ryan, Kate. "'A new day': Prince George's County education leader on reopening schools." WTOP News. Last modified July 6, 2020. https://wtop.com/coronavirus/2020/07/a-new-day-prince-georges-county-education-leader-on-reopening-schools/.

plagiarism (and the administration told me I shouldn't be so tough even when the entire paper was a cut-and-paste job from Wikipedia), I wouldn't grade on a curve, and I wouldn't give easy As and Bs for poorly written papers. The top students would say, "Pat Brown is the best professor I have ever had," and the poor or failing students would say, "Pat Brown is the worst professor I have ever had." What the college wanted was for professors to "go easy" (read: grade inflate and allow plagiarism) on their students so as to keep lazy, overly busy, incapable students paying for the programs. Some students who took online classes with me worked full-time, had a full five-class schedule, and had two small children at home. They actually told me they could only give about two or three hours a week per class. Unbelievable! But, if professors "helped them out," then they could pass all five and the college could keep the money coming in, even if the students were hardly learning a thing. Professors learned quickly if they wanted to keep their jobs, they had to be "nice."

I refused to give in, and I was let go. My fifteen-week courses were shortened to eight weeks, and material removed by people who were not at all familiar with criminal profiling. The certificate program still exists, but I no longer can recommend it to anyone because I know that the program I developed is long gone and its replacement is some watered-down travesty. And yet, there are professors teaching it in spite of the fact they are not competent to do so, and they are willing to do so even if they have to essentially forgo all quality to get the students through. No ethics, no problem. Professors of all people should never stoop to this. But where is the outcry? Where are the conservatives fighting back against the destruction of our education system? We need more voices out there.

Likewise, with the media, especially television. I did over three thousand appearances in my media career, but I started fighting back when the whole industry descended into fake news. The last CNN show I did was on November 29, 2015. Here is the *NewsBusters* article that details exactly what happened and why I took the stand I did, a stand that effectively ended my relationship with CNN.[3]

> It was one of those stunning live-TV moments revealing the seamier side of TV news. Pat Brown is a criminal profiler who has taken a principled stand on media appearances about mass murderers. She will not discuss individual criminals, their motives, etc., believing that to do so only increases the number of mass murders.
>
> But when Brown appeared on CNN's New Day this morning, co-host Christi Paul immediately tried to engage her in a discussion of Colorado Springs shooter Robert Dear's possible "anti-government" views. Retorted Brown: "I'm a little disturbed because I made an agreement with CNN to appear this morning only under the condition that we do not talk about the particular shooter, use his name, or show his face." Undeterred, Paul tried to lure Brown into a discussion of the shooting investigation, but again Brown rebuffed it. There the interview ended, but co-host Victor Blackwell came on to claim that the agreement had been honored because neither Dear's photo nor name had been used. Didn't use Dear's name? Really? Have a look at the screencap, Mr. Blackwell.

---

3.   Finklestein, Mark. "Crime Expert Rips CNN On Aire for Dishonoring Agreement Not to Discuss Colorado Shooter." NewsBusters. Last modified November 29, 2015. https://www.newsbusters.org/blogs/nb/mark-finkelstein/2015/11/29/crime-expert-rips-cnn-air-dishonoring-agreement-not-discuss.

View the video and watch CNN get called out on its bait-and-switch invitation to Brown. It's ironic that Brown thought she had an agreement to discuss the way the media has contributed to the recent tripling in mass murders by giving the murderers such attention. And then CNN proceeded to try to do just what Brown has been complaining about. Talk about adding insult to injury!

CHRISTI PAUL: I want to bring in criminal profiler Pat Brown, she's the author of "Killing for Sport: inside the minds of serial killers." Now, I want to make it very clear we are not characterizing him as a serial killer. But this is Pat's field of study and her expertise, and Pat, I know that a neighbor said the suspect gave him an anti-government flyer. Let's listen to what this neighbor had to say about the suspect.

NEIGHBOR: They were nice, really nice guy, you know? Talking to us and everything. Gave us some anti-Obama flyers, little pamphlets and I didn't even really read them. I just -- I think I used them to start the fire in our camp fire that night.

PAUL: And again, there are reports that he did say some things that seemed to indicate an anti-government view to investigators since his arrest. What does that specif-ically -- you know, that background on him tell you, if anything?

PAT BROWN: Well, I'm a little disturbed because I made an agreement with CNN to appear this morning only under the condition that we do not talk about the particular shooter, use his name, or show his face. Not to talk about the particular mass murderer. I do not do that. I took a stand three years ago not to talk about individual mass murderers because I believe we in the media are increasing the number of mass murders. It has tripled in the last decade and it's my belief that the notoriety we give them does this. And I came on this morning to talk about the media's role and responsibility in stopping talking about the mass murderers. We don't need to that. They are the same mass murderer every time. All we need to say is this: an attention-seeking, psychopathic loser has committed a heinous crime and we're not going to talk about any him any more. The motive is always the same: power, control, and attention in the media. And that is what we are giving him every time we talk. We need to stand down as a country and say we don't need to hear any more about these mass murderers. We're just going to stop talking about them. We are not going to name them, we're not going to show their face and we're not going to sit here and discuss forever and ever and ever what his motive is because it doesn't matter. He's a horrible criminal. He has committed a heinous crime. Put him away and that is the end of it.

PAUL: Okay, and I understand that. And I respect your views on that, surely. But we certainly can talk about the investigation into what is happening, can we not?

BROWN: No, we cannot. I specifically said I will only come on if we don't talk about this individual mass murderer. We do not need to do that. That is my stand for three years. And I was surprised actually that I got to come on this morning because in three years I've given the same statement and I've been turned down for three years and I was so happy that CNN was going to let me come on and talk about the media's role and responsibility and the increase in mass murder and so thank you for that but I'm sorry we didn't stay with the topic that I came on to talk about.

PAUL: All right. I understand. I respect your views. And I thank you for coming on.

BROWN: Thank you.

VICTOR BLACKWELL: Let's be clear, and let me read from the e-mail from Pat Brown. Here's the quote. Is my segment free of any photo or name of the mass murderer? That segment did not have any photograph nor use the name of the suspect and we held to that agreement.

The Washington Post naturally took a slightly less positive view of my stand. Their headline was "CNN guest blows up interview over mass killer media ethics" and states "things got unhinged fast," and how the host tried to "salvage" Brown's appearance (as if it needed salvaging). The reporter, Erik Wemple, went on to ask, "[W]hat can we say about someone like this?" He kindly said I did helpfully address some issues, but then at the end concluded the whole interview was absurd and the media outlets should have total license to talk as much as they like about serial killers. This gives serial killers the notoriety they love and encourages them to kill, which was the entire reason I refused to kowtow to the host's questions.[4]

---

4.   Wepile, Erik. "CNN guest blows up interview over mass killer media ethics." *The Washington Post.* Last modified November 30, 2015. https://www.washingtonpost.com/blogs/erik-wemple/wp/2015/11/30/ cnn-guest-blows-up-interview-over-mass-killer-media-ethics/.

To be fair, it was the producer who screwed this up. She promised me something and failed to inform the host. But, regardless, I felt I had to stand my ground and I did. It didn't do wonders for my career, but I still feel it was the right thing to do. Problem is, it is difficult to get folks to stand up when their careers are at stake. I, fortunately, had no young children at home to feed, but if one does, it makes it all the more difficult to fight back. This is one reason Trump supporters have often been afraid to even admit they supported Donald Trump because it could destroy their livelihood.

But what of larger organizations? Why are large conservative organizations often not doing what they should? Have you all been wondering how my lawsuit against Meetup turned out? What? You haven't seen anything in the media about it? Wouldn't a major conservative legal organization going to court against Meetup for violating the Civil Rights Act of 1964, for discriminating against whites, wouldn't you have seen that big news story in all the papers and on all the media channels? At least on the conservative ones?

Yeah, you would if there *was* a lawsuit in progress. I tried and tried to get legal representation. Naturally, I had to go to the ACLU first because they are the civil rights organization of note. I believe they turned me down because they are no longer about equality but pushing a leftist agenda. I expected this outcome.

But what shocked me is that I have been unable to get *any* conservative legal group interested in representing me against Meetup. I rather thought that after appearing on *Tucker Carlson* I would get a phone call from an interested party. I got lots of wonderful emails and phone calls from citizens cheering my efforts but not one phone call from any organization willing to go to bat against racism against a white person. I called and emailed many organizations and never heard back from any. Maybe I missed the one that would have gone to court for me, and maybe I will hear from that one organization now that this book has been published, but up until this date, I have had no response.

I have talked to private attorneys, and I discussed at length with my favorite attorney how good a case I had against Meetup. He believed, after doing research, that my case was excellent. In spite of this being a new arena, online business and advertising as opposed to a bricks-and-mortar location, the Civil Rights Act of 1964 would appear to support my case as these groups that are advertised via Meetup are public accommodations just like a restaurant, a gym, a store, or a club. But, sadly, because the attorney told me the likelihood of a large settlement was very poor (I hadn't suffered a loss of income or a crushing blow of any kind), he could not represent me on contingency. And because Meetup is a very big organization with a lot of money, I could hardly afford to pay the attorney fees to move forward. Hence, the need for pro bono work from a major conservative rights organization.

Why is there so little interest from these organizations? Is it because there is too little money to be gained by representation, or is discrimination against whites an issue even conservative groups don't want to touch for fear of backlash?

But if we don't stand up in court, in education, in the media, or in elections, conservatives will lose this country to a very liberal, socialistic way of life. And there may be no way to recover.

AFTERWORD

STEP FORWARD

WHAT TRUE AMERICANS CAN DO
TO SAVE THEIR COUNTRY

> "History will have to record that the greatest tragedy
> of this period of social transition was not the strident
> clamor of the bad people, but the appalling silence of the
> good people."
>
> Martin Luther King, Jr.[1]

PAT

When Dave and I started writing this book in the beginning
of 2020, President Trump had improved the economy fantas-
tically and he was winning the fight against impeachment.
We were concerned about the racism and separatism we saw
growing day by day, but we never saw the major hit our country
was going to take with the arrival of Covid-19 and the death of
George Floyd. As is pointed out by political scientists, revolution is most possible when a country is in economic crisis.

From the time we started writing *Black and White*, the
country careened quickly downhill into an almost unrecog-

---

1. Mindock, Clark. "Martin Luther King Jr: 50 quotes from the civil rights leader
who inspired a nation." *Independent.* Last modified January 20, 2020. https://
www.independent.co.uk/news/world/americas/martin-luther-king-quotes-death-
assassination-mlk-jr-a8855071.html.

nizable state, a land of such insanity and continuous change. People started joking how they were so old they could remember February 2020.

So what has occurred in just the short time we were readying our book for the publisher?

Another black man, Rayshard Brooks, was shot and killed during an attempted arrest in Atlanta, Georgia. The protests started immediately and this case (added to the George Floyd case) was proof in their minds that racism in America was indeed systemic.

However, this case took the rush to justice one step further. In spite of video of the man resisting arrest, attacking the police officer, and stealing his stun gun—and in spite of this man seen turning and firing that stun gun at the policeman (which was when he was shot and killed)—protesters claimed he was murdered and the DA charged Officer Garret Rolfe with felony murder.[2] The police had become the enemy of the black people and "defund the police" became the battle cry. Budget cuts started coming in, police quit or retired, and new recruits were difficult to come by. Crime began to rise sharply in cities around the country.[3]

And this second uprising over a videotaped killing by police of a citizen seemed to become the expected reaction to any such event, regardless of whether or not it was a justified homicide by police. On August 23, 2020, another young black man, Jacob Blake, was shot in the back during an attempted arrest by police officer Rusten Sheskey of the Kenosha Police Department in Wisconsin. Headlines immediately blasted across the

2. Bynum, Russ, Lisa Mascaro, Jim Mustian, Matt Ott, and Sudhin Thanawala. "Atlanta Officer Garrett Rolfe charged with murder for shooting Rayshard Brooks." KUSI News. Last modified June 17, 2020. https://www.kusi.com/atlanta-officer-garrett-rolfe-charged-with-murder-for-shooting-rayshard-brooks/.

3. Crime and Justice News. "With Crime Rising, Budgets Cut, More Officers Retire." The Crime Report. Last modified July 13, 2020. https://thecrimereport.org/2020/07/13/with-crime-rising-police-budgets-cut-more-officers-retire/.

media depicting Blake as an innocent unarmed black man just trying to get into his car whereupon he was gunned down in front of his three children. Riots ensued to the point where it felt like Minneapolis all over again. Businesses were burned and violence erupted on the streets to the point where two people ended up dead. But, then it came out that Blake was no innocent; he was the reason the police showed up after receiving a call for assistance, he had open warrants out on him, and he did resist arrest. He was tased and this did not work to quiet him. Then, he reached into his vehicle when told to stop and the police officer, fearing he was accessing a weapon (a knife was later found on the driver's side of the car), opened fire.[4] Many police officers have been killed by an "unarmed" man who managed to then get hold of a weapon and take the officer down. But, neither the media or the public felt a need to wait for the facts to come out; the incident was another occasion to push a political agenda. And, when it gains traction, the truth seems to fade away. Why less than a week after Blake was shot, his father, Jacob Blake, Sr., appeared with Al Sharpton at the 2020 March on Washington claiming his son was a victim of racism, of a two-tiered justice system.

> There's a White system and there's a Black system. The Black system ain't doing so well, but we're going to stand up. Every Black person in the United States is going to stand up.
>
> We're tired. I'm tired of looking at cameras and seeing these young Black and brown people suffer.[5]

4. Astor, Ashley. "State on Blake shooting: Tasers were ineffective, one officer fired all 7 shots." FOX 11 News. Last modified August 28, 2020. https://fox11online.com/news/state/doj-releases-more-details-on-blake-shooting.

5. Hanna, Jason and Harmeet Kaur. "Jacob Blake's sister at March on Washington: 'Black America, I hold you accountable.'" Last modified August 28, 2020. https://www.cnn.com/2020/08/28/politics/march-on-washington-black-national-convention-trnd/index.html.

Never let a good opportunity go to waste.

Along with the protests against specific police-involved shootings, the issues of discrimination and systemic racism spread like a cancer throughout communities, schools, sports, and businesses. It seems nothing was left untouched. Statues of historical figures the Left found offensive were vandalized and destroyed while mayors told law enforcement to stand down and allow the crimes to be carried out. Then, mayors across the US gave governmental approval to the painting of Black Lives Matter down the main streets of cities, allowing for political messages of one particular group to be supported by the local government. So far, no mayor has approved a MAGA painting on any street.[6]

Oh, and remember how in Spike Lee's movie, *Do the Right Thing*, it was considered racist to not have any photo of famous black people on the walls of a restaurant serving the black community? Well, in Washington, DC, a Jewish Deli took down their photo of a famous black singer and a burger they had named after a famous black rapper underwent a name change. Why? Because it was considered cultural appropriation and exploration of black people to make money.[7] Damned if you do, damned if you don't.

And what of the fabulous Broadway musical Hamilton? The one celebrating the life of Alexander Hamilton, one of the founders of our nation, the one with a cast of all people of color? The one the black community raved about just a couple

---

6.   Matthew, David. "California town scrubs Black Lives Matter mural after Trump supporter requests 'MAGA 2020' painting." *New York Daily News*. Last modified July 21, 2020. https://www.nydailynews.com/news/national/ny-redwood-city-black-lives-matter-mural-trump-maga-mural-20200721-pbpvpd7l5bbftoq6q3z5qfrk5e-story.html.

7.   Iannelli, Nick. "Popular DC deli apologizes for 'co-opting Black culture." WTOP News. Last modified June 30, 2020. https://wtop.com/dc/2020/06/dc-deli-apologizes-for-co-opting-black-culture/.

of years ago? Now, it is being "cancelled." After the stage version was filmed by Disney and made available through streaming on the Internet, the attacks came fast and furious that the show was too nice to white people and didn't show them in an evil enough light, that slavery wasn't more featured, and that the show had the audacity to cheer the founding of our country and the men who made it possible.

What else has happened? Already ADOS (American Descendants of Slavery) seems to be a term thrown by the wayside in favor of BIPOC (Black and Indigenous People of Color). But, give it time, a new name might be in instituted by the time this book is published in 2021.

Attacks on whites became more frequent and there was a change in the atmosphere of the majority black county where, up until now, I never felt any discrimination. For the first time, I experienced negative and rude attitudes toward me that clearly had to do with the color of my skin. If I bring up this issue, I am immediately called a "Karen," an entitled white woman boohooing because she got her little toe stubbed. "Karen-calling" is a great way to dismiss someone's concerns and make their opinion irrelevant. If a white woman wants to avoid this situation, it is far easier to join the Left, believe in what they say is correct to believe in; an odd sort of Stockholm Syndrome situation where white women, and many white men, become psychological prisoners of the Left.

Meanwhile, it is odd that white intellectuals are on the forefront of the Black Lives Matter movement, telling blacks what to think! And energized by a feeling of power injected by way of the media, the protests, white allies groveling, marching and rioting in the name of racial justice and black power, many American blacks see their Wakanda rising—that fictional black kingdom with the Marvel superhero Black Panther—and there is shouting of "Wakanda Forever!" Only the country won't be located in Africa but will be the new America once the revolution overturns the power structure. Even Pharrell Williams isn't *HAPPY* anymore and he has gone from singing how nothing can bring him down and clapping and dancing with all races to stating that the protests sweeping the nation have him finally feeling like an American and that "we must trust in a Black vision of the future." [8]

And this is the mindset that carried over to the Democratic National Convention (DNC) during the last half of August. In a train wreck of a four-night infomercial, I watched in horror as speaker after speaker claimed our country was a disaster—not from the coronavirus or the racial hatred or the violence across our cities—but because we have never been a good country and Donald J. Trump is proof of that. Oddly, the most uttered word of the convention was "empathy," and the entire platform of the party seemed to have nothing to do with any policies but rather with holding hands and being empathetic—although to whom that empathy is being extended is quite questionable. I certainly have felt little empathy from the Left over the last decade. The only real empathy I saw extended was toward Joe Biden as each one of the failed candidates, including Kamala Harris, did an about-face and said he was the most wonderful, hardworking, and, of course, empathetic man who has ever run for President of the United States.

But, the very next week, the Republican National Convention (RNC) actually gave true hope to the citizens of this

---

8.　　Reapers France, Lisa. "Pharrell Williams: 'We must trust in a Black vision of the future.'" CNN. Last modified August 21, 2020. https://www.cnn.com/2020/08/21/entertainment/pharrell-williams-racism-essay-time/index.html.

country. I was spellbound, glued to the proceedings, and I have never watched much of a convention before. The speakers were far more diverse than what the DNC gave us during their convention. Imagine that! Blacks, Latinos, Asians, women of all colors, immigrants, the young, the old, the disabled, Christians—even a nun—those who were pro-life and those who were pro-2nd amendment. The successes of Donald J. Trump during his presidency were detailed and his plans—the specific plans he had for the future—were laid out. I learned a tremendous amount of what the platform of the Republican Party under Trump was going to strive to accomplish if we are fortunate enough to have President Trump win a second term. It was truly magnificent and I felt I was watching what America was all about; citizens who loved their country, public servants who actually wanted to serve their country, and, at the end of the four days of positive speeches, each ending with "God bless America," came our President, Donald J. Trump with as presidential a speech as one could possibly imagine. I was blown away. For the first time in my life, I could actually say, "I love my President."

If radical progressivism wins the day, the far Left of the Democratic Party and, these days, perhaps, a good portion of the rest of the Democratic Party, will have their goals fulfilled. It won't be the country our founders envisioned in which "all men are created equal" and it won't be the dream of Martin Luther King, Jr., with whites and blacks holding hands and sharing equally in a better America. No, our United States will not be that any longer, but will instead be a land of apartheid, separation, and tribalism—the kind of place where Marxism can make itself at home for decades to come.

We cannot let this happen.

DAVE

Every great civilization in human history has come to end. Some slowly burned out like the Roman Empire and others descended quickly into chaos and annihilation. I often wonder how the citizens of those civilizations perceived their last days. Was it expected? Did they see the decline coming? Or did they wake up one day and finally come to the realization that what they took for granted had evaporated before their eyes? If America was on that slow descent, 2020 has seen us catapulted forward into chaos and madness. At times it seems surreal. Cities being burned, businesses being looted, with little push back from authorities. In fact, elected officials in some cities are egging it on, siding with the rioters over law enforcement. That does not shock me. There are nutjob mayors and nutjob governors who slither their way into public office. What does confound me is the apathy and encouragement of suburbanites. Middle- and upper-class people post a black fist on their Facebook page to show solidarity with Black Lives Matter. Soccer moms have become weekend social justice warriors, cheering on the mob. Has history taught us nothing? Violent mobs are like a raging wildfire. Where and when they turn to wreak havoc and destruction is erratic. Today they may burn down the inner city, but tomorrow they could be marching into your suburban cul de sac.

Watching the DNC and RNC conventions could not better highlight the two paths America has before it. On one hand, we have the Democratic Convention. Hoping to highlight the dysfunction thrown upon our society by the coronavirus, the DNC decentralized the entire process. Ironically, a party that enjoys uniform support of Hollywood put on what amounted to an online high school Zoom production. The participants joined the convention remotely with disjointed pre-taped segments. Live shots were awkward and mistimed. Interludes were filled with grating musical interludes preaching clichéd and forced messages of racial unity. And to top it off, their nominated candidates were the two most cynical picks that the Washington DC Establishment could have coughed up.

Joe Biden joined the Senate in 1973. In 1988 and 2008, he would run for president. Both attempts ended in colossal failure with accusations of plagiarism and lying.[9] In 2008 however, he was selected to be Barack Obama's running mate. At the time, there was speculation as to why Obama would pick Biden. The best reason given was that he was a safe, white face. An old white backdrop behind the first black candidate for president. As to whether or not it actually worked, who knows. But the eight years as VP did give him some prominence. Even so, he declined to run in 2016. Partly because the slot was already designated for Hillary Clinton, and in part because no one took him seriously. That changed in 2020, when a field of radical and unknown Democrats vied for the nomination. Washington, spooked by the prospect of have an unknown and perhaps radical quantity running for president, pulled Biden off the scrap heap. Long in the tooth, and arguably showing signs of dementia, they threw him up as a last-ditch effort to have someone they could control run for office. To top it off, he (or his handlers) selected Kamala Harris as his running mate. Another former candidate for president who flamed out miserably during the primaries—most notably in the debates.

Why? Well, she is "black," although during her swearing in ceremony at the Senate, it was her Indian heritage she chose

9.   Perticone, Joe. "Flashback: Joe Biden's First Presidential Run in 1988 Cratered amid Multiple Instances of Plagiarism," *Business Insider*. March 12, 2019. https://www. businessinsider.com/plagiarism-scandal-joe-biden-first-presidential-run-1988-2019-3.

to highlight. Like most politicians, she is whatever she needs to be at the moment. During the 2020 debates, she was one of Joe Biden's most ferocious critics, accusing him of both hurtful positions on race and of committing sexual assault.[10] She "believed" the women that made the accusation. Later, when asked how she could make such an about-face and join his ticket, she laughed it off. "It's politics" she exclaimed. "Politics!"[11] An empty skirt to complement the empty suit beside her. What was their 2020 platform? Orange Man Bad! How inspiring.

Thankfully, we were able to chase that bad taste out of our mouth left by the DNC convention with the RNC—professionally shot on a beautiful stage with the White House as a backdrop. The message was refreshingly pro-America with a focus on our strengths, not a rambling screed about every conceived ill endured throughout our country's history. The event reached its zenith with President Trump's acceptance address. A hopeful vision for America with economic and personal security for all. The speech concluded with an amazing array of fireworks and to top it off, opera sung from the balcony of the White House. Trump's America is one of hope, patriotism, and limitless growth.

Those are our two paths. America the Beautiful, or the clown car that is the Democratic Party. It feels as if the fuse has already been lit, the die cast, and that civil war is descending upon us. The election will be long past when this book is

---

10. Kevin, William B. "Kamala Harris Attacks Joe Biden's Record on Busing and Working with Segregationists in Vicious Exchange at Democratic Debate," CNBC. June 28, 2019. https://www.cnbc.com/2019/06/27/harris-attacks-bidens-record-on-busing-and-working-with-segregationists.html.

11. Mandel, Bethany. "Kamala Harris Believed Joe Biden's Accusers - until She Didn't." *New York Post.* August 12, 2020. https://nypost.com/2020/08/12/kamala-harris-believed-joe-bidens-accusers-until-she-didnt/.

released. God willing, Donald Trump will be serving four more years giving us further opportunity to push back and right this ship. If not, despite my dislike of his person and lack of confidence in his stewardship, I pray that Joe Biden will provide some stability in these times of uncertainty. Regardless of the outcome, our duty as patriots continues and persevere, we must.

PAT

President Donald J. Trump was our "Mr. Smith goes to Washington."[12] Unlike the naïve fictional Mr. Smith, who had no idea what he was getting into when he stood up against the corruption that was the order of the day in Washington, DC, President Trump knew he was walking into the lions' den, and he did it anyway—for the American people. He showed us what was really happening in our capital and around our country. Whether one agrees with or likes President Trump's approach and personality, no one can say that he didn't expose the belly of the political beast and what was happening in our political parties that was tearing our country apart. No matter who is in the White House in 2021, it is up to us citizens to work on bringing our country together—all of us from all colors and subcultures—to be the Americans our forefathers wanted. In the words of Martin Luther King, Jr., "The time is always right to do what is right."[13]

---

12.   "Mr. Smith goes to Washington." Wikipedia. Last modified July 29, 2020. https://en.wikipedia.org/wiki/Mr._Smith_Goes_to_Washington

13.   Mindock, Clark. "Martin Luther King Jr: 50 quotes from the civil rights leader who inspired a nation." *Independent.* Last modified January 20, 2020. https://www.independent.co.uk/news/world/americas/martin-luther-king-quotes-death-assassination-mlk-jr-a8855071.html.

ABOUT THE AUTHORS

PAT BROWN is an internationally known criminal profiler who has worked many cases in the US and abroad. She has over 3,000 media appearances on television cable news and radio, having appeared regularly for years on NBC's *Today Show*, *The Early Show*, *FOX & Friends*, *Tucker Carlson Tonight*, *Nancy Grace*, *Jane Velez-Mitchell*, and *The Joy Behar Show*. She runs The Pat Brown Criminal Profiling Agency and is working to develop training in profiling for police agencies. She has written six  books and developed the first Criminal Profiling Certificate Program in the United States. Always a middle-roader in political matters, she became far more conservative during the Obama years. She supported Donald J. Trump in his presidency and believes that we can Make America Great Again if only we stop dividing the country and painting half of our citizens as racists and bigots. She has a master's degree from Boston University in Criminal Justice.

DAVE BROWN has always been interested in politics and economics, studying at the University of Hawaii and the University of Madras in Chennai, India. He received his BA from Thomas Edison State College. He owns his own solar company and works as a project manager in construction. He is biracial with his father hailing from Jamaica. He is a conservative and wants to inspire other blacks and people of color to join in Making America Great Again.